INTERNATIONAL
MANAGEMENT

To order additional copies, please contact us.
BookSurge, LLC
www.booksurge.com
1-866-308-6235
orders@booksurge.com

SUSIKU AKAPELWA

INTERNATIONAL MANAGEMENT

Principles & Applications
First Edition

2005

INTERNATIONAL MANAGEMENT

TABLE OF CONTENTS

ACKNOWLEDGEMENTS

As one might expect, compiling any text entails a great deal of effort and as such, I offer my many thanks to all those I have benefited from their insights and knowledge. I also wish to acknowledge my alma maters, Troy State University and Slippery Rock University of Pennsylvania for extending their capabilities. It would be remiss of me not to mention my present and past employers as well as the many business associates I have dealt with for the wealth of knowledge bestowed upon me. My appreciation to Jenny Legan, senior publishing consultant at Booksurge publishing for her efforts.

Last but certainly not the least, I extend my thanks and continued appreciation to my rock and foundation, my dear parents, Mr. Simataa Akapelwa and Mrs. Margaret Sitwala Ngula Akapelwa, family members, my love and joy as always to my angel Susiann. Despite my utmost best efforts, I accept responsibility for any shortcomings within the text and welcome any suggestions, comments or corrections from readers, however I trust the rewards and personal fulfillment offered by the text overshadow the shortcomings and offer an invaluable resource. To everyone and each of you, this humble work I dedicate.

Sus

Akapelwa Financial Group
Ft. Lauderdale, Florida 33324
Phone: (954) 530 5964
E-mail: sus@akapelwa.com
Website: www.akapelwa.com

PREFACE

I first felt compelled in writing a book primarily for instructive and research purposes four years ago. At that time, I had four essential driving considerations and motivations for taking time to compile a text: (1) Present the student at undergraduate and graduate level a supplemental tool with a simple, plain and concise approach toward understanding the many intricate applications of management, finance and economics without wasting time with long drawn out nuances. (2) Offer a text that students, researchers, and general readers alike can use as a research source and more importantly, enjoy. (3) Introduce readers to the many fascinating aspects and opportunities of economics, international management & finance. (4) Incorporate and share my expertise in the field of financial management, strategic planning, economics, and International management through my analytical reviews which are open ended like many issues a professional in the global arena will encounter, thus allowing the reader to absorb the presented materials and draw their own analytical insights.

One might ask, why the emphasis on international management? The answer is fairly straightforward; in today's world, we live in an environment that is so interconnected in all facets. Business entities are no longer confined to local municipalities, regions or national boundaries, but rather, are structured to operate on a global framework. We have all heard of "Outsourcing", China and India come to many peoples mind. Therefore, the renaissance business professional in this new millennium is required to be astute and cognitive of both the internal operating factors as well as the external environmental forces in the global arena. Today's successful international management professionals understand the importance of acknowledging and reacting to internal & external factors, be it political or environmental forces. They intuitively understand and can relate to cultural differences, and more importantly are cognizant to the ever-changing global playing field. The global business arena has manifested what I phrase as the "E" factor, **excuses, execution** and **excellence,** very important concepts to say the least. Successful multinational managers invariably show excellent execution strategies resulting in excellent achievement where as mediocre managers are at a standstill buried with excuses resulting in poor results.

Terms such as globalization, multinational companies (MNCs), transnational management entities and so forth are as prevalent as management 101 in the business sphere. The arena is wide open with the most brilliant open—minded professionals at the top of the hierarchy. The subject mater pertaining to international management collectively mirrors all variations of commerce and collectively translates to the subject matter of international management. The impact of globalization forces can be felt and seen across the globe, this enormous force is here, we have two pragmatic decisions to circum to; embrace the phenomenon or contend with the manifestations. At best as professionals, we need to examine and employ the tools at our disposal and thus the essence and core of this text.

ORGANIZATIONAL STRUCTURE

The structure of the book incorporates both principles and applications in the field of international management, however the scope of the materials and subject matter within the text is not only limited to principles and applications but rather covers detailed practical analytical overviews for each section. The reader is exposed to the broad range of overt and underlying concepts of international management with real world practical analytical overviews.

The opening chapter presents an introductory overview of basic international law concepts and applications, examining its sources and motivations. State sovereignty and treaty law concepts are examined, as is the issue of human rights. Emphasis is devoted to the United Nations as a body and it's role in international law. The next chapter offers the reader a perspective of the international economy, drawing attention to trade issues, outsourcing, market structures, exchange rates and a host of other concepts. Chapter 3 transitions into global management strategies at play within the global arena and gives some insights on how Multinational Company's strategize & implement plans. Chapter 4 outlines the U.S. Labor Relations laws laying emphasis on early labor developments and follows with descriptive as well as procedural applications. Chapter 5 is dedicated to financial analysis; the section has useful definitions, working examples and formulas key in financial analysis. In chapter 6, the focus is on ethical behavior in business, examined in this section are code of ethics, corporate governance, free-trade and other principles in the business environment, the issue of globalization and its manifestations is revisited within this section. Chapter 7 looks at general principles of organizational behavior and also devotes wide attention to notable pioneers in management thought. The closing chapter offers an overview of intercultural communication and its pivotal role in the whole scheme of things' addressed in this section are conflicts in dialogue, worldviews, cultural and gender issues, negotiation and a host of related issues.

As the sub-title indicates, this is a text strong on principles and applications, the core of the material is centered on descriptive concepts and how such concepts are applied in the international business environment, it is therefore my hope that reader's will digest and employ the materials as best as their needs and competencies allow.

CHAPTER I
International Law Overview

1.0 State Sovereignty in the Modern Context

State sovereignty in the modern context is essentially aligned with the 1933 Montevideo Convention on rights and Duties of states as provided in article 1 of the UN charter. In accordance with these provisions, the modern outlook on sovereignty follows four main criteria's listed below as a stipulation for state sovereignty.

a). Permanent population

This stipulation entails the physical permanent presence of human beings cohabiting in an established community regardless of their differences in terms of religion, beliefs, etc. The essence of this notion primarily calls for an established population group sustaining as one community regardless of any sub-cultures present within the larger group.

b). Defined territory:

This ideal calls for not only having and possessing a territory, but rather more important is the ability to have ownership and control of such territory, therefore just occupying a territory without valid ownership and control could be a disqualifier to the general doctrine of state sovereignty. (It is important to note that an occupied state within a state may exist, however whether or not such an entity is recognized as a sovereign state under international law is a different issue.)

c). Government Structure

A functional government with authority to effectively manage the population and the accompanying territory is the third stipulation. This condition calls for both internal stability and external cooperation with the international community, therefore a state cannot only expect to meet its internal governance and forego international established parameters. Exceptions could be raised when a state takes action based on what it perceives as a threat to its core existence as a sovereign state.

d). Capacity for agreements & negotiations

Relates to a nation being capable and able to carry out interactions with the international community through treaties, conventions, tribunals, and common good for all parties.

1.1 Principle of State Responsibility

The principle of state responsibility allows for nations to act reasonably and within the accepted principals of international law. This includes but is not limited to honoring signed treaties, agreements, declarations and so forth. Deviating from compliance will put a state into a conceivable breach of international law. Actions against violators are not uniform and for the most part tend to be very cumbersome and bureaucratic, however the most common approach is associated with imposition of sanctions.

1.2 Conditions making a Treaty Binding

The traditional framework calls for "conclusion and entry into force of treaties" as spelled out in Article 9 of the 1969 Vienna convention. Two principle provisions within the article articulate the following stipulations:

a). Adoption of a treaty will call for agreement by all parties or states putting forward the initiative, i.e. consent amongst the parties

b). Adoption of the treaty will follow a vote of two-thirds of the participating states.

Article 11 further expounds on this notion focusing on the expression of a treaty by means of signature, ratification and accession as the main stipulations. Also included in this reading as binding conditions are acceptance, approval or any other agreed upon criteria amongst the states. (goes to show how broad the criteria of binding a state to a treaty could be stretched.)

Modern practices have also utilized other mechanisms as pointed out below:

a). Exchange of correspondence between states

b). Open ended treaties (Article 83)

c). Acceptance or approval instead of ratification

d). Treaty drawn by international body.

Conditions making a treaty non-binding

a). Provisions for termination met by all parties involved

b). Mutual consent by parties

c). Breach by one of the parties involved

d). Treaty failure or collapse

e) Change in circumstances from those initially agreed upon

f). New customs or new view in international law framework (implies a change in worldview)

1.3 Nature of state succession

Stems from the notion of change in sovereignty as regards to territory. Key considerations point to which rights and obligations of the precluding treaties are recognized or nullified. International law to begin with is very ambiguous in this area and therefore, this area of international law lacks clarity. Recent examples include the Yugoslavia disbanding and the disintegration of the USSR, which resulted in numerous, fragmented states having conflicting notions of which treaties to recognize.

What Motivates States to Establish IGOs?

- Enhancement of the states influence as a coalition building party.
- Security concerns
- Economic motives
- Increased economic interdependencies
- Capitalization of raw materials
- Humanitarian objectives
- Protection of human rights
- Environmental concerns, nuclear proliferation concerns, transportation and communication issues.

Legal status of IGOs in world affairs and legal rights and responsibilities

IGOs operate within the constraints and binding objectives of the respective member states, as such the legality of IGOs is a function of the member governments. IGOs in some instances are capable of proclaiming judgments.

1.4 Purpose of the United Nations

a). Promote and maintain international peace and security across the globe.

b). Develop friendly relations among nations

c). Cooperate in solving international economic, social, cultural and humanitarian issues.

d). Promote respect for human rights and freedoms.

The UN carries out these functions through its six principal organs, namely the: General Assembly, Security Council, Economic & Social Council, Trusteeship Council, International Court of Justice and Secretariat.

Status of General Assembly Resolutions in International Law

Resolutions passed by the general assembly can have a quasi status of international law by serving as tribunal hearings for settlement of disputes, such decisions though binding lack the authority to bring an individual state before a court without it's consent.

UN operating as a collective security arrangement

The UN utilizes its various operational wings to achieve this goal. The General Assembly and the Security Council are the prominent tools in collective security. The General Assembly as body allows for all member states to convene and deliberate on motions of concern patterning to issues of threats, security, human rights etc. Members cast votes and can condemn a state as being in violation to agreed upon principles. In such a manner, the UN through the General Assembly exhibits a collective security arrangement. Another means is through the Security Council where binding decisions can be made to states in the interest of international peace and stability. Actions can also include sanctions, embargos, military intervention and so forth. All these actions through the Security Council entail a collective security arrangement, as the ultimate goal is collective global security.

UN practice under Chapter VII of the Charter After the Cold War

After the Cold War, the UN has had more room and flexibility to engage in broader causes such as human-rights agendas. An increase in humanitarian engagements such as the Dafour, Somalia crisis have been undertaken by the UN. The UN has also been more actively involved in various peacekeeping missions. The UN role also took a turn after the 911 catastrophes in the US, the 911 attacks put the UN at the forefront as did the Iraq & Afghanistan conflicts. The post-90s have seen a greater role by the Security Council.

International law governing the use of force by nations

The simplistic notion for use of war today by states follows the premise of acting in self-defense or protecting a states territory, inhabitants, resources or interests. However, as we all know, the decision to use force is not a simple matter but rather a very complex decision requiring utmost thought. As such, international law through history has struggled with this issue; the last centaury has seen an attempt to translate customary rules into multilateral international agreements. Examples include The Geneva Convention (1864), The Paris Declaration (1856), The St. Petersburg Convention (1868) and The Hague Peace Conference (1899 & 1907). All these agreements combined form a framework in guiding the use of force by states today. Whether they are effective or not is a different matter altogether. As mentioned earlier, these agreements were early protocols, today's international law protocol relies mainly on post WW II initiatives embodied in the UN charter. The international community in concert seem to all agree upon these stipulations as detailed in the UN charter. The four cornerstone rules justifying use of force are outlined as follows:

1. Right to self-defense when attacked (armed attack)
2. UN Security Council enforcement
3. Enforcement actions by regional organizations authorized by the Security Council
4. Peacekeeping e.g. ECOWAS forces in West Africa

Is Terrorism a violation of international law?

The context of this question presents one with a two-fold answer, allow me to expound; "Attacks carried out on civilians who take no part in hostilities are prohibited by international humanitarian law" as spelled out in the 1949 & 1977 Geneva Convention protocols. Thus a terrorist act that follows such manifestations could conceivably constitute a violation of international law in theory and practice. Having said this, the dynamics of terrorism are always not this cut & dry. Terrorism by nature has been a tactic employed through history, as events would testify, a reference point could be made in the American colonist actions against the British where terror tactics were employed. The key underlying question and dilemma when discussing terrorism is the lack of consensus as to what constitutes terrorism. Often, terrorism and freedom fighting cross paths and in many cases mirror each other, each acting as means to an end to each other, indeed so often, one man's fight for freedom can be construed as another man's fight against terrorism. The issue of state sponsored terrorism across the globe as one might anticipate presents a distorted gray area, which is often overlooked by international law, and for that matter general law. Given the ambiguity involved, this question remains very convoluted.

State sovereignty's continued role in international law?

The relationship between state sovereignty and international law is clearly not a new phenomenon but rather one that dates back centuries. The dynamic though not new has seen several transformations over the different periods of time, one constant being that the two ideals are intertwined to varying degrees. Recent changes in the global structure particularly with the demise of the cold war and the onset of globalization has naturally changed the role each plays. This section will thus examine the modern role played by sovereignty in international law with primary emphasis on post—cold war influences, nation invasions, sanctions, failed states, human rights and NGO groups. However, before exploring the above-mentioned themes, a brief overview follows.

The theory of sovereignty dates back centuries with prominent theorists such as Machiavellian, Jean Bodin, Thomas Hobbes and John Austin at the forefront. In fact, John Austin defined law as the general commands of a sovereign state and went on to proclaim that international law was not law since it did not align with his theory [1]. Subsequent shifts in international law readings associated the notion of sovereignty generally as an independent state but not above the law. [2]. This theory continued to evolve over time through the classical era which saw the emergence of the basic principles in international law centered on territorial sovereignty, control over territory etc., however not included in these principles was the right for a state to go to war to protect it's sovereignty. [3]. Other developments relating to human rights protection would eventually follow as well as influence by international organizations such as the Hague peace conference of 1899 and 1907. [4]

POST COLD WAR INFLUENCE

The sudden collapse of the soviet union and effectively the diminishment of the cold war brought a whole new set of dynamics in the global arena as long established allegiances between east vs. west were crumbling. With effectively only one super-power left, that being the United States, the United Nations took on a bigger role in conflict resolution across the globe while the United States for the time being retreated and took a back seat. [5]. The permanent members of the Security Council took on a more prominent role in mediating and in some cases making demands over sovereign states. Clearly the prominent role taken by the UN showed a new shift in the relationship between sovereignty and international law given the UN as an instrument of international law. In many cases, fragile sovereign states on the brink of collapse non-the less still considered sovereign states worked in concert with the UN in resolving their conflicts thereby circumventing chaos and destruction. Such was the case in Africa where the withdrawal of Cuban troops was successfully negotiated between the parties and, as was the case with the withdrawal of soviet troops in Afghanistan. [6]. Other eventualities and mediations followed, however these two situations are just a few circumstances of sovereignty playing a role in international law and vice versa for that matter of fact.

IRAQ INVASION OF KUWAIT

The invasion of Kuwait by Iraq in 1990 is a classic example of sovereignty playing a dominant role in international law. Saddam Hussein, the leader of Iraq at the time felt it within his sovereign right to invade Kuwait as he deemed it a part of Iraq territory and therefore justifying his invasion of that nation. The international community through the auspices of the United Nations Security Council saw Saddam Hussein's action as unacceptable and lacking merit therefore calling for the immediate withdrawal of Iraqi forces from Kuwait. The tug of war went back and forth with a series of resolutions, which were ignored by Iraq. Subsequently, Iraq was given a deadline to pull its troops out of Kuwait or face consequences. In this instance, we see a state defying an international order in Resolution 67 and facing the consequences of the order spelled out under the international order.

IMPACT OF FAILED STATES

Somalia presents a scenario of a failing sovereign nation where the international community through the UN had to intervene due to catastrophic humanitarian concerns. The UN organized food aid through various agencies and a multinational coalition of over 37,000 was deployed to restore law and order. Other collapsing sovereign states such as Rwanda, Yugoslavia and so forth have also played a role in international law through international courts of justice to bring perpetuators of heinous human war crimes to trial. In these incidents, former accused leaders such as Melosovich and the former head of state of Rwanda were tried under international court tribunals. Haiti is another case of a crumbling sovereign state where in this situation the sitting president was actually forced out by the international community (mainly the U.S.) in order to restore law and order. Sovereign states that infringe on their subjects human rights also play a crucial role in international law. Such abuses are monitored by the International Law of human rights under the UN umbrella. [7]

As we draw to the end of this section, we have seen a few instances of sovereignty interacting with international law in a variety of ways. Indeed the scenarios examined just represent a fraction of the other various manifestations, however one can clearly see that the issue of sovereignty and international law can be very complex and uncertain. It's an ever evolving dynamic, as has been illustrated from the earlier periods of the classical international law era to the present where we see a wider role played by international coalition bodies such as the UN and the wider scope of treaties. I see this situation even taking a greater role as we dig deeper into this globalization era where the world is interconnected and thus sovereignty taking less significance going forward.

REFERENCE NOTES

1. Malanczuk, Peter, AKEHURST'S Modern Introduction To International Law, 2004.pg17
2. Malanczuk, Peter, AKEHURST'S Modern Introduction To International Law, 2004. Pg17
3. Malanczuk, Peter, AKEHURST'S Modern Introduction To International Law, 2004. Pg 19
4. Malanczuk, Peter, AKEHURST'S Modern Introduction To International Law, 2004. Pg22
5. Malanczuk, Peter, AKEHURST'S Modern Introduction To International Law, 2004. Pg395
6. Malanczuk, Peter, AKEHURST'S Modern Introduction To International Law, 2004.pg402
7. Weiss, Forsythe, and Coate R., The United Nations and Changing World Politics, 2004. Pg129

1.5 UN tools for achieving security in the world

The United Nations employs a variety of branches within its organizational body in achieving order and security across the globe. The nature and scope of influence exerted through such tools is the primary focus of the latter part of this section. Also addressed will be the different roles of the UN in the post-cold war as opposed to its role at its founding in the pre—world war II period. The concluding part of the section will look at the prospects of the UN serving as a vehicle for maintaining world order after the cold war.

The Security Council is a critical tool the United Nations has at its disposal for attaining world peace and order. The core function of the Security Council as spelled out in the Charter is to promote and maintain international peace and security. Other auxiliary functions of the Security Council include but are not limited to, investigating disputes, reconciling settlements, recommending & imposing sanctions, and military action against an aggressor state. Given such a broad realm of responsibilities, the United Nations inherently treads diplomatically and assumes an indirect approach. [1]. When such an approach proves futile, the UN begins to take a more forceful approach, as some examples later will show. Typically, the Security Council steps begin with a complaint brought forward concerning a perceived threat to peace, at this juncture the Security Council recommends to the parties involved to try to reach an agreement using peaceful means. [2]. If a peaceful truce appears unlikely, the UN can further utilize Chapter VII of the charter therefore binding the parties in question. When the UN takes such a decision, given an established link between human rights and security, then economic or military action is a possible consequence. [3]. This expression of influence by the UN was utilized in conflicts in Rwanda, Sierra Leone and the former Yugoslavia. The UN also uses non-binding measures in certain instances, as was the case with South Africa in the late 1970s. At that time, South Africa was in the grip of the Apartheid system and the Security Council in 1977 voted for an arms embargo against South Africa on the basis of people's denial of self-rule and majority rule [4]. This tool was earlier used in the case with Rhodesia (now Zimbabwe). The UN may also impose economic sanctions through the Security Council to deal with a state posing as a threat to peace as was the recent case in the 90s with the "Food for Oil" embargo against the Iraqi regime. When a conflict ensures, the Security Council can opt to send peacekeeping troops to bring the conflict to an end, this measure has been used recently in conflicts in Africa.

Another arm the UN relies upon in securing global peace and security is the General Assembly. This body consists of all member states representatives with each member having one vote. The primary function of the General Assembly is to deliberate and pass resolutions promoting international peace and stability. Included in this definition of responsibilities is the promotion of human rights, therefore the General Assembly also condemns acts that are in contrast to the promotion of basic human rights by casting up and down votes. This practice can be very embarrassing for the condemned state in violation therefore could result in such a violator making amends to their practices. The UN can also use The Office of the Secretary—General as a useful tool. Secretary—Generals may take an active role in an area that is of interest to them such as human rights or refugee issues and bring that to the forefront. By virtue of the stature of the office itself, the exposure a Secretary-General brings over an issue is an invaluable tool in itself. Koffi Annan has been an overwhelming crusader for the plight of human rights. [5]. The UN High Commissioner for Refugees, The UN High Commissioner for Human Rights, The Human Rights Commission and other auxiliary bodies are also additional tools the UN utilizes in achieving order and security in the world. These bodies are particularly influential in creating stability and order in areas where human degradation can easily erupt into potential chaos and anarchy.

UN Mission Post Cold War

In today's Post-Cold war era, the role of the UN has evolved from its earlier mission following the World War II period. The Cold-War period was an era of enormous tensions between the East-West powers, which created a high degree of isolation with lesser emphasis on internationalized solutions to conflicts. Given the Cold-War tensions, the two main superpowers (USA & The Soviet Union) were consumed with maintaining and building their ideologies. This situation meant the UN played a lesser role in conflict resolution and pursuing it's set objectives. The end of the Cold War in turn created many fragmented states particularly in the former Soviet bloc and other nations that had allegiances and financial support from the USA & Soviet Union. This manifestation, particularly the Soviet collapse also resulted in new internal conflicts in the newly independent states such as Yugoslavia, Bosnia as well as other states such as Cambodia, Angola and so forth. The collapse of such states is also significant in the new emergent role of the UN in that; the Soviet Union for instance had expended a vast amount of resources sustaining the Cold-War to the extent that by the time the Cold-War ended, it's treasury and resource base was greatly diminished. Under the leadership of Mikhail Gorbachev, the Soviet Union sought to take a new direction and revamp it's economy and become more integrated into the world economy. In fact, Grobachev called for a renewed relationship with the UN at the General Assembly in 1988 in resolving global conflicts. [6]. This renewed world outlook in conflict management called for the UN to take a more active role in peacekeeping campaigns in failing states from the cold-war collapse. This view was not only echoed by the Soviet leadership but also shared by the U.S. Leadership. Both President Ronald Regan and later on President George Bush made similar sentiments calling for the UN to capitalize on this opportunity and play a bigger role in global conflict management. This renewed vigor toward the UN gave the organization new legs in the pursuit of new post Cold-War commitments. The biggest change in the post Cold-War period for the UN was its increased role in peacekeeping missions. Between 1988-1993 alone, the UN engaged in five military operations after a ten-year absence. [7]. With the vow and commitment from the U.S. and the Soviet Union to pay their dues to the UN, the organization was also able to engage and undertake in more humanitarian causes. The Gulf War in the early 1990s gave the UN a forum to play a very visible role on the world stage. The Security Council for the first time since 1950 unanimously condemned the invasion of Kuwait as violation to world peace. [8] The UN voted to use economic sanctions against Iraq and passed a critical resolution,"678" allowing for "all necessary means" to remove Iraq from Kuwait. The September 11 tragedy in the U.S. and the resulting invasion of Afghanistan and Iraq also thrust the UN again in addressing state sponsored terrorism and nuclear proliferation. In essence, the UN post Cold—War has seen a rise in Peacekeeping & humanitarian missions and has actively followed it's objectives of creating norms against violence, create international stability, and pursue humanitarian concerns.

The prospects of the UN to serve as a vehicle for maintaining world order now that the Cold War is over offer mixed results. While the UN has clearly increased its role in this era, measuring the results of such efforts presents a challenging and complex dilemma, however one thing that seems clear is that with the world becoming so intertwined in this era of globalization, more challenges are inevitable. The global poverty disparity is widening in places with vast populations such as Africa, and given such poverty proportions, one can expect and foresee ethnic conflicts such as we have seen in Rwanda, Somalia, Liberia, Sierra Leone, and many other parts of the world. In summation, this section has illustrated that the UN evolves with times and as such, one can expect it to continue serving as a vehicle for world order, however the issue of success and failure of its pursuits remains an open ended matter with varying interpretations.

REFERENCE NOTES

1. Weiss, Forsythe, and Coate R., The United Nations and Changing World Politics, 2004. Pg153
2. United Nations. (2005)
    www.un.org
3. Weiss, Forsythe, and Coate R., The United Nations and Changing World Politics, 2004. Pg155
4. Weiss, Forsythe, and Coate R., The United Nations and Changing World Politics, 2004. Pg156
5. Weiss, Forsythe, and Coate R., The United Nations and Changing World Politics, 2004. Pg16
6. Weiss, Forsythe, and Coate R., The United Nations and Changing World Politics, 2004. Pg47
7. Weiss, Forsythe, and Coate R., The United Nations and Changing World Politics, 2004. Pg48
8   Weiss, Forsythe, and Coate R., The United Nations and Changing World Politics, 2004. Pg5

1.6 Human Rights and International Law.

The issue of human rights as relates to international relations have long being intertwined and the very notion of extending entitlements to legally protect individuals, minorities, & indigenous groups from state interference or abuse in many cases is in contradiction with the states concept of sovereignty. The origins of the concept of human rights has paralleled the development of today's modern state. One can look back at the early Western governments and find that human rights concerns were echoed in the American and French revolution. Such early intrusions of human rights concerns were very limited in scope and had little or no impact outside their immediate domain. The 19th century saw an explosion of human rights concerns on the scene with Karl Marx at the epicenter of this development. The 1890 Brussels signing by Western countries to abolish the slave trade was another landmark moment in the ever-developing concept of human rights with regard to international affairs.

However, the watershed turning point of human rights and international law took root after World War II. Prior to WW II the international community was more concerned with engrained ideals of maintaining their individual sovereignty and as a result, human rights issues were typically viewed as matters to be dealt with internally within each sovereign state. This mode of thinking and approach changed following the events that transpired in WW II. After the brutal holocaust events subjected on Jews by Nazi Germany, the global community realized they could not just sit and let such atrocities go by simply as an internal matter. This in essence brought the issue of human rights to the forefront and thus allowing for a new approach. Central to this new approach regarding human rights was the United Nations. The UN Charter under Article 1 elevated human rights as an issue of utmost importance. Article 55 spelled out this global respect for human rights and freedoms. Article 56 further reaffirmed this commitment calling for all members to pledge their support in achieving the goals stipulated in Article 55.

The commitments addressed in Article 55 and 56 are ideally supposed to bring international law in concert with human rights in protecting the vulnerable, and as earlier pointed out, there has indeed been an increased emphasis on matters pertaining to human rights which is in direct contrast to classical traditional international law, non the less that has been the trend. Also significant is the reaction and attention the pro human rights approach attracts, i.e. cries from governments of interference within their internal matters. The dilemma lies in the fact that most states still view issues pertaining to their own nationals as an internal matter and vehemently oppose any interjection by outside forces proclaiming existing human rights violation. Most states would seem to be more supportive of human rights pursuits as long as it does not apply to their internal circumstances therefore bringing another problematic issue of double standard. The nation of Zimbabwe recently has been internationally castigated as violating human rights with its demolition of squatters and political intimidation of opposition members.

Another troubling issue that crops up when dealing with human rights issues are engrained cultural, economic and political differences that exist across the globe. This is particularly significant because these differences make it virtually impossible to come up with a universally accepted notion of human rights definition. As such, each state is compelled to say that under their cultural norms and ideals, an act viewed, as a violation of human rights or suppression of freedoms is perfectly normal and within their constitutional and sovereign right. In fact, some go as far as arguing that the whole notion of human rights protection lacks any international legal protection or basis. It is important to note that many positive commendable strides have been made as a result of this new aggressive approach of pursuing and enforcing human rights abusers globally, however the seeming contradictions lead us to the underlying question; is this issue of human rights intruding over old legal concerns a solvable issue? Due to the increased interdependences in today's globe and enormous advances in technology which allow for instant access of alleged human rights violations in our living rooms via satellite TV, internet etc, the prospects of this issue being solvable are very good because world perspectives are more in concert, for instance a perceived violation is beamed all over the globe and if this is a valid issue it becomes very difficult to deny the allegations against a global audience in the name of the states sovereign right.

Human rights can be accommodated within international law through the various bodies of the UN. The UN views severe human rights violations to be dealt with through international channels. The International Court of Justice is also obligated to take up matters concerning severe human rights violations. Recent examples where we have seen human rights violations channeled through international law include the violations in Rwanda and the Melosovich trial. Thus said, as complicated and difficult this subject matter of human rights and international law presents, the overall outlook seems positive however long the journey may take.

CHAPTER II
THE INTERNATIONAL ECONOMY

2.0 Arguments for free trade

Proponents of free trade or open markets in the classical economist era argued that such a practice was a force in promoting the international division of labor since it allowed for nations to channel their competitive edges on goods they could produce at the cheapest cost thus resulting in specialization of production. The rationale for this thinking lays emphasis on the notion that each nation to a degree has inherent competitive advantages such as climate, mineral endowment, and skills. Utilizing such given natural competitive advantages thus fosters free trade. Early economists such as Adam Smith pointed out the principal of "labor theory of value" which implies labor as a homogeneous factor cost and thus the cost of goods being contingent on the labor pool required to produce a given good. Smith further argued using a simplistic 2 nation, 2-product ideal called the "principal of absolute advantage" that trade was most beneficial when one country has an absolute comparative advantage. Given all these arguments, the cumulative effect is said to be higher consumption and investment while consumers enjoy lower commodity prices.

Arguments against free trade

Adversaries of free trade point out that nations tend to impose trade restrictions in the form of quotas and tariffs against foreign imports. In addition to protectionism, arguments against free trade imply that such trade promotes outsourcing and dumping of cheap products, which in turn can result in an imbalance of trade. Local jobs are also threatened as production facilities are relocated and thus could create unemployment.

Factors fostering rate of growth after WWII.

After WWII holocaust nightmares, there was a renewed collective embrace by the international community to move forward and this in turn created a globalization wave from the mid 1940s to the early 1980s.

The current ongoing surge in free trade began in the early 1980s in part due to some developing nations breaking the ranks of LDCs and becoming newly emerging economic forces, this was particularly evident with the far-east Asian "Tiger" nations. Countries such as Malaysia, Thailand, China and so forth were a big driving force in this trend. Other factors can be attributed to technological and information advances, ease of mobility, and a more liberalized environment (NAFTA, GATT).

Impact of changing supply-and—demand conditions on international terms of trade

Shifting supply and demand conditions creates an interesting dilemma on traditional international terms of trade in the sense that enforcement of such terms is almost impossible and the propensity to violate labor practices is very likely. Trying to police unfair trade and labor practices globally is a very challenging proposition.

2.1 Alternative Trade Theories

Leontief Paradox challenge toward the overall applicability of the factor endowment model

The Leontief paradox undermined the conclusions drawn in the factor endowment model by using empirical studies in 1947 and 1954. Wassily Leontief's investigation followed the assumption that since the United States was recognized as having abundant capital and relatively scarce labor, it should follow according to the factor endowment theory that the United States would export capital intensive goods and import labor intensive goods. Given this premise, Leontief analyzed over 200 capital and labor ratios of export/import competing industries, his findings in contrast to the factor endowment model found that the capital/labor ratio for U.S. exports was lower than that of competing import industries.

Differences between the Heckscher-Ohlin theory & Ricardian theory in explaining international trade patterns.

The Heckscher—Oblin theory implies that factor endowments are the source of comparative advantage among nations where as the Ricardian theory states that the source of comparative advantage is contingent on relative costs.

Theory of overlapping demands.

Staffan Linder's theory of overlapping demands contends that factor-endowments play a pivotal role in world trade that involves primary products, natural resources & agriculture goods but has no implication in the global trade of manufactured goods. The theory uses the rationale that the main driving force in the trade of manufactured goods is domestic demand since manufacturers will tend to manufacture goods which have a large domestic market, and the overflow of such goods are exported to nations with similar consumer tastes. In essence, the theory implies the export or trade of manufactured goods an extension or function of domestic production.

2.2 Trade barriers and Non Trade barriers:

Specif Tariff

Expressed in fixed monetary terms per physical product imported without regard to value or quantity of imported item. Advantages of such a tariff include its simplicity and relative ease in application, its ability to shield domestic producers in times of a recession when consumers buy cheaper domestic products than more expensive exports. Main disadvantage lies in the fact that protection of local producers has an inverse relationship with import prices.

Ad Valorem (of value) tariff

Expressed as a fixed percentage of the value of imported good.

Advantage: tariff inherently distinguishes product quality assuming there is a correlation between price and quality. This type of tariff also offers consistent protection to local producers, as price fluctuations do not affect its effectiveness. The tariff also offers revenues that are proportionate to the value of goods.

Disadvantage: determing value (customs valuation) of imported good can be cumbersome. Variations in methods used to determine a goods value, e.g. U.S. uses free on board (FOB) while Europe follows the cost-insurance-freight (CIF).

Compound Tariff

Applied to manufactured products that contain raw materials subject to tariffs.

Advantage: protects local suppliers of raw materials and consequently promotes manufactures use of local materials.

2.3 Trade blocs and Trade policies for Developing countries

Trade liberalization existing on a non-discriminatory basis versus a discriminatory basis

Non-discriminatory form: relationship involves a mutual agreement by parties involved to have a reduction of trade barriers on a nondiscriminatory form. A good example is the World Trade Organization

Discriminatory form: this relates a group of nations forming regional trading arrangements among themselves e.g. NAFTA, COMESA, EU

Common Agriculture Policy as a controversial issue for the EU

This policy created a problem for the EU because of the differences in production efficiencies amongst the farmers within the union, for instance, German grain farmers had higher production costs than French farmers, therefore under the EU's price-support program, countries with lower efficiency costs have lobbied for high support costs even though not necessary, but rather as a free benefit. This as such has created inefficient farm production.

Generalized system of preferences

This initiative is intended to help developing nations gain access to world markets by offering non reciprocal tariff relief or preferences to exports from developing countries in order to allow such countries an opportunity to enter the global trading market while strengthening their manufacturing base.

2.4 Adam Smith's view on international trade & that of the mercantilists.

The center piece of Adam Smiths view of international trade was the notion of free trade (open markets) unlike the mercantilists view during the period of 1500—1800 which stipulated that in order for nations to obtain a positive trade balance, they had to put in place Tariffs, quotas and other prohibitive measures. Adam Smith called for free trade stating that such an approach would promote international specialization resulting in each nation producing goods they were most efficient at producing. Adam Smith justified his theory with the principal of cost differences being the driving force in production, therefore some nations may have natural advantages such as mineral wealth, special skills, labor supply and so forth. Smith's theory is founded on two principals; labor theory of value and absolute advantage. Therefore, the underlying difference between Smith and the Mercantilists is trade restrictions vs. free trade.

2.5 Conditions necessary for a developing country to establish a market economy

a). Market—determined prices/ Open economies

Prices are not controlled or manipulated by the government or a central body but rather are self determined with the forces of demand and supply. Price is the driving force and consumer's ability to purchase goods and services determine the price levels. No state planning and control of foreign and domestic trade. (open for debate.)

b). Independent Buyers and Sellers with property & legal rights

Buyers and sellers need to be able to operate in their own interest without any coercion or intimidation, these two entities are the driving force of the market economy. In essence, buyers and sellers need an environment where they can trade openly and have their vested property and legal rights.

c). Stable governments with limited role in economy

A developing country also needs a stable government with a laissez faire approach in order to foster an open market otherwise market failures arise under oppressive or intimidating conditions.

d). Good Fiscal and monetary policy

Developing countries need stabilized currencies and avoid erratic fluctuations, high inflation, and overall poor monetary/fiscal policies.

2.6 Outsourcing.

Outsourcing can take many forms, it could be a company delegating some of its functions to a subcontractor, it could also involve the transfer of jobs or certain function capabilities overseas or it could follow a company relocating part or the entire production process offshore. Outsourcing could also be domestic, an example could be a financial institution with its headquarters in Boston delegating the functions of collections on delinquent accounts to an outside unrelated collection company operating in Atlanta.

Benefits of Outsourcing

1. Promotes competition among global companies, as the cost margins of firms are reduced due to relatively low labor and factor costs associated with outsourcing.

2. Increased competition and reduced factor costs in turn translate to lower consumer prices, the consumer is therefore left with more disposable income which is reinvested back in the economy resulting in creation of more jobs and an overall expanded economy.

3. Outsourcing is a driving force for innovation; due to the increased

competition, companies are forced to constantly develop new products in order to maintain or gain a competitive edge.

4. Outsourcing brings an opportunity for new exports because as income levels rise in host countries such as India and China, the consumers in those markets are able to afford new products that may not be readily available in their country therefore fostering exports.

Disadvantages of Outsourcing

1. Loss of jobs in communities where production facilities and functional units relocate from
2. Potential to drive wages down
3. Exploitation of laborers in developing nations as labor laws offshore may be difficult to enforce

2.7 Steps toward Economic Integration

Economic integration refers to the process of removing restrictions on international trade, payments and factor mobility. A classic example of integration is the European Union. Outlined below are the steps followed for integration.

1. Removal of tariffs and establishment of a free-trade area.
2. Customs uniformity
3. Elimination of non-tariff trade barriers such as border control and customs red tape.
4. Formation of common Central Bank, e.g. European Monetary Union (EMU). This is typically parallel with steps toward a new currency.
5. Convergence, i.e. the alignment of economic and monetary policies to bring involved countries on a similar economic performance threshold.
6. Full fledged economic integration.

World Trade Organization (WTO) rules for commercial conduct of trading nations

1. Membership provision required since the WTO is an international organization
2. Members still required to uphold GATT rules affecting trade pacts negotiated under GATT auspices
3. Members required to be committed to unified package of agreements administered by the WTO

4. WTO reserves the right to reverse policies of protection in critical areas such as agriculture and textiles
5. Member nations free to set their own environmental, labor, health and safety protections.
6. Disputes by member's states administered through numerous councils and committees of the WTO
7. Agreements by member nations pertaining to tariff cuts and reduction of non-tariff measures are implemented by the WTO.
8. Members trade practices are regularly examined by the WTO; member states are also required to update their trade statistics that are maintained by the WTO database.
9. Trade in services; intellectual property and investment are included in the multilateral trading system.

2.8 Payments among nations & the foreign exchange market
Balance of international indebtness & balance of trade

Measures the level of international investment of the United States, essentially weighs the value of U.S. investments abroad versus foreign investments in the United States. This is a measure of both short and long term investment positions of the private and public sector of the economy. It is not however a measure of debt owed. Balance of international indebtness differs from balance of payments in that it compares levels of investment abroad vs. foreign investment in the United States where as the balance of payments is a record of a country's economic transactions with other countries in a given year.

Forward market & Spot Market

In a forward market, currency is bought and sold now for future delivery, with the delivery time typically being 1 month, 3 months or 6 months from the transaction date. In a spot market, currency is bought and sold for instant delivery usually two days after the transaction.

What factors underlie currency exchange values in a free market?

Market fundamentals, this includes economic variables such as productivity, inflation rates, real interests rates, consumer preferences and overall government trade policy. Market expectations also play a role in currency exchange values, by this we mean things such as news of future market fundamentals and general trader opinions or speculation about future exchange rates, essentially chatter among traders.

Factors that apply to short-run exchange rates (few days to weeks)

Dominant factors are transactions involving transfer of financial assets (bank deposits), these transfers respond to variations in real interest rates and future expectations of exchange rates. The medium-run (several months) is greatly driven by cyclical forces within the economy

Factors that apply to the long-run exchange rates (1—5 yrs)

Primarily determined by investment capital inputs & the flow of goods and services. These variables respond to forces such as inflation rates, investment returns, consumer preferences and government trade policies. Long-run value changes to the exchange essentially are a result of exchange trader responding to four factors:

A). Relative Price Levels

B). Relative Productivity Levels

C). Preference for Domestic or Foreign Goods

D). Trade Barriers

Monetary approach to exchange rate determination addresses the shortcoming presented by the two traditional approaches (elasticities & absorption), which do not associate monetary consequences of balance of payments adjustments. The monetary approach contends currency depreciation can contribute to the balance of payments standing.

Factors affecting exchange rate movements:
- Employment levels
- GDP
- Level of business activity
- Deficits
- Other macroeconomic variables

Government's main role in rate determination:

The government's principal role essentially is to intervene in adverse periods when the foreign exchange markets show a great deal of volatility which could hurt the economy in the long-run, whether this is a good practice or not is debatable, my view is that government intervention in rate exchange markets if used only in dire situations serves the populous a greater benefit.

Managed Floating Exchange

Managed floating exchange rates are determined by forces at play within the free-market, essentially demand and supply forces with occasional minimal government intervention through the Central Bank. Managed floating rates are governed by informal guidelines established by the IMF, these guidelines are used for coordination of national exchange rate policies. The guidelines also address two major concerns, the first involving nations intervening in exchange markets in order to circumvent exchange rate movements that might weaken their currency position. The second concern relates to disorderly or erratic market fluctuations, therefore member states can intervene on the exchange markets to prevent sharp erratic exchange rate movements from day to day and month to month.

Managed floating exchange rates were adopted by industrialized nations in 1973 following the breakdown of the international monetary system, which was based on fixed rates. Managed floats operate under the underlying concept of a "clean float" which translates to a market rate determination as opposed to a "dirty float" which refers to the practice of not letting the free-market forces of supply and demand achieve their equilibrium role.

Perfect capital mobility and the effectiveness of monetary and fiscal policies under fixed exchange rate.

Under a fixed exchange rate system, perfect capital mobility means having a measure of controls on capital movements, such controls are also referred to as exchange controls. These controls are government imposed in order to support fixed exchange rates and prevent speculative attacks on currencies.

Fixed exchange rates and developing countries

Fixed exchange rates are good for developing countries because it provides for a stabilizing effect since currency markets in most developing countries are still a work in progress and thus can be very volatile. Fixed rates also present an opportunity for the government to somewhat control capital flows, this is important for developing countries in that the government can influence its payments position. Developing nations government's can therefore encourage or discourage certain transactions by offering different rates for foreign currency for different purposes which can be of critical importance for developing country.

2.9 Zambia's Transition Toward An Open Market Economy.

Introduction

Zambia is a landlocked nation located in central southern Africa, eight countries namely, Tanzania, DRC, Malawi, Namibia, Angola, Mozambique, Botswana and Zimbabwe border it. The land area covers 752,614 square kilometers. The most recent census figures put the population figures at 10 million. The country's GDP was listed at $4.1 billion according to figures from 2003. Zambia has one of the highest urbanized population rates in the Sub-Saharan region with the figure estimated to be at 46% [1]. The principal city and commercial capital is Lusaka (pop 1.5 million). Other major cities include, Ndola, Kitwe and Livingstone. Copper and Cobalt exports account for 77% of export earnings and the remaining primarily agriculture and tourism. Average daytime temperatures are 15-27 Celsius. Zambia is a country with an enormous amount of mineral resources with copper dominating, other minerals include, zinc, lead nickel, uranium, coal, gemstones, gold, etc. Zambia is however internationally recognized as a major copper and cobalt producer. Since the 1920s when copper production began, the social and economic fabric has heavily relied on this industry.

The primary purpose of this analytical review is to explore and examine the steps Zambia has embarked towards becoming an open market economy. The review will address some of the strategies employed by the Zambian government and point to some successes as well as failures.

Dawn of open market forces

The early 1990s in Zambia were dominated with a hive of activity centering on the dawn of democracy, for the first time since the country's independence in 1964, multi-party elections were in full swing. The country had been governed by the strong hand of its founding president, Dr. Kenneth Kaunda since independence under a one party state, and for the first time the prospect of a new government regime was not just a buzz but seemed rather an eminent reality to come. A new government would in fact be elected into power bringing the principles of democracy to this nation, underlying this democracy movement were sweeping economic implementations intended to move Zambia into a free enterprise open market. This paper examines the strategies and objectives undertaking toward achieving this goal.

Mission

"Successfully transition Zambia from a government owned parastatal economic structure to a full fledged open market economy with underpinnings of capitalism."

Objectives and Strategies Matrix

Objectives	Strategies
1. Increase Investment Activity	Liquidate government parastatals into private holdings
2. Increase productivity and job opportunities	Sell Mining Assets, the backbone of Zambia's economy, over 80% foreign revenues
3. Reduce Inflation Rate to less than 18.5%	Sound monetary policy compounded by cumulative effect from above mentioned strategies
4. Stabilize exchange rate (Market Determined)	Improved foreign reserves as a result of favorable export earnings due to high metal prices
5. Boost tourism	Advertising campaign through Visit Zambia awareness drive to attract western tourists
6. Increase Real GDP	Agriculture, mining, tourism and manufacturing
7. Poverty Reduction	Agriculture, mining, tourism and manufacturing as driving forces

Implementation of strategies & objectives

Mining and Manufacturing strategies:

Declining world copper prices, inefficiencies and the ailing mining infrastructure had taken its toll on the entire industry with production numbers at their lowest output. In the mid 1990s, the Zambian government began a full-scale drive to privatize the Zambian Copper mining industry. Bids and tenders were formally put out to the public and major mining companies began to line up and submit bids, the process as one might expect was long and drawn out with a lot of red tape and bureaucracy. In 2000, the Zambian government had completed the comprehensive privatization of the Zambian copper industry. After dismantling the massive Zambia Consolidated Copper Mines Company, which was the ninth largest copper mining company in the world, the mining sector was completely privatized with foreign companies.

Tourism and Agriculture sector:

The strategy to boost the agriculture sector was to target Zambia as a potential major grower and exporter of agriculture and horticulture produce. The selling point to investors was the vast abundant quality arable land, very good climate and a relatively good transportation network. The Zambian authorities realized how much underutilized their land resource was, of the 60 million hectares of arable land, only 15% was being cultivated. [6]. The government strongly encouraged commercial farmers by offering them incentives that in some cases were tax induced to get these farmers to relocate to Zambia. The campaign attracted hundreds of commercial farmers from South Africa and Zimbabwe (many whose farms had been seized by the Mugabe regime).

In the tourism area, Zambia implemented an advertising initiative called the "visit Zambia campaign", this campaign was to showcase all of the abundant natural beauty and wildlife the country had to offer, the target market for this marketing campaign were Europe, U.S.A & the Far East. The pivotal aspect of the campaign was promoting the Victoria Falls, which is listed as the 7th wonder in the world, the campaign was also designed to coincide with the 100th (centennial) anniversary celebrations honoring David Livingstone who founded the Victoria Falls in the town of Livingstone, Zambia. The government also felt its 19 National Parks & 34 Game Management areas were untapped. [7].

Observations

Strengths:

- Mineral natural resource endowment & energy resource
- Vast arable unutilized land
- Relatively strong human capital resource
- Stable government
- Pleasant climate
- National park system & Victoria Falls (seventh wonder)

Weaknesses

- Underutilized natural resources
- Underutilized tourism
- undiversified economy, too much reliance on copper reserves
- Unemployment too high & Poverty constraints
- Poor health system

Opportunities

- Capitalize on rising world copper prices
- Increased tourist visitation
- Commercial agriculture sector expansion
- Manufacturing sector virtually non existent

Threats

- AIDS epidemic
- Erratic world copper prices & subsequent copper substitution
- Shaky democracy
- Unpredictable exchange currency rate
- High urbanization, poverty and unemployment
- Brain drain, too many professionals relocating to the Western countries and neighboring southern African countries such as Botswana & South Africa where better wages and opportunities present themselves.

Concluding Remarks

The trade liberalization moves undertaking in Zambia towards its quest to be a full fledged open market economy have had mixed results. The single most important strategy naturally involved the privatization of the mining industry. The new multinational companies that now run these mines for their part have pumped in millions upon millions of dollars in infrastructure enhancements, which have resulted in efficiencies and production being boosted. World copper prices have also appreciated on the commodities market in the last few years. On balance this objective has been a plus for the Zambian nation even though it needs to pay attention to employee union issues regarding wage compensation. Recent employee strikes could be a concern, however to their credit, the multinational companies responded swiftly with a 30% wage increase to mine workers which settled things down. Another worrying issue with the multinational mining companies has been the spate of mine accidents where mine workers were killed underground in failed shafts and explosions, such incidents caused alarm in the mining region because they had not occurred at such a frequency with the government owned mining companies.

Macroeconomic objectives have been very positive, GDP has continued to grow the last four years largely attributed to favorable world copper prices and improved efficiencies and production levels. Inflation levels have also shown marginal declines but have rather been offset by food price inflation increases, so while this objective has been somewhat met, a lot of work needs to implemented in the area of food prices, this was also largely impacted with low maize (corn) yields due to droughts. It is imperative that the government also redirect their focus on commercial farmers to encourage them in producing consumer crops such as grain rather just paying to the higher paying cash crops such as tobacco. Other potential underutilized sectors are manufacturing and tourism, these areas offer vast foreign exchange potential. The AIDS pandemic is very worrisome, perhaps the biggest constraint Zambia faces, and all resources need to be allocated in order to overcome this threat. It's a good start for Zambia in its journey to a free-market economy, however, the journey is also proving to be long and bumpy.

REFERENCE NOTES

1. http://usembassy.state.gov/zambia/cguide.html
2. www.glencore.com
3. Anglo American Fact Sheet
4. US Geological Society
5. www.mining.co.za/copperbelt
6. http://www.boz.zm/Economics/economics_main.htm
7. http://www.boz.zm/Economics/economics_main.htm

CHAPTER III
GLOBAL MANAGEMENT STRATEGY

3.1 MNCs and changes in the global environment

Changes in the international operating environment have had a drastic effect on MNCs and consequently a shift in global management strategy and general approach by MNC managers. These external changes have involved political, social, economic and technological forces. On the political front, many host governments have increased their level of restrictions and demands on MNCs. In many instances, host governments have applied pressure on MNCs to invest and transfer technology locally, required greater local management involvement and in some rare cases insisted on part ownership arrangements. Adding to this constraint for MNCs, local customers at times have looked at global products with disdain and their calls for national products have increased.

In view of such political & government forces, MNCs have recognized the importance of responding to such local forces. MNCs have realized that the need to respond to local forces was synonymous with their goals to remain globally competitive and efficient. This observation resulted in many MNCs following what's referred to as the "transnational" strategic mentality. This approach allowed companies to shift their main activities from a centralized base and instead focus on each international market, as it's own self-sustaining operation performing its functions on a localized basis. By employing such an approach, the MNC to a certain degree is able to respond to growing government and local forces while also maintaining its global competitiveness. Since the transnational approach lays heavy emphasis on domestic level operations unlike some of the earlier global strategy, managers of MNCs have been able to deal with other environmental factors such as social and cultural differences.

The impact of globalization particularly in the 1990s meant MNCs had to re-evaluate their operations to ensure optimal global integration and coordination. Some of the forces driving this phenomenon included factors such as economies of scale, economies of scope, factor costs and a liberal global trading environment. As such, MNCs had to respond to each force appropriately to remain competitive, for instance, the resulting economies of scale in many cases drove companies to outside markets in order to remain competitive. Collectively, all the above-mentioned forces in large part contributed to MNCs enhancing their global coordination so as to optimize their global competitiveness. However the biggest influence to the globalization drive could be attributed to the liberal environment for global trade, NAFTA for instance is good case in point. Technological advances also played a role in driving globalization forces, the product life cycle was reduced due to these resulting technological advances, which meant that only those companies adapting to worldwide innovation could gain a global edge. In response to all these forces, MNCs enhanced their global operations by specializing their production process, standardizing parts design, specializing the manufacturing operations and other measures. MNCs also increased their research and development budgets for developing products on a global scale.

3.2 MNCs and Structural Fit

The first part of this section devoted attention to the changes within the international operating environment and how these very changes made MNCs adjust their global efficiency structures, responded to localized forces and engaged in worldwide learning. Naturally, all these responses and adjustments are channeled through the MNC management structure. The second part examines the assertion that the basic problem underlying a company's search for a structural fit was that it focused on only formal structure and that this proved to be unequal to the task of capturing the true complexity of the strategic task facing most MNCs. Indeed this notion of finding a "structure fit" consumed managers in the earlier years and in fact for most managers, this way of thinking became the norm rather than actually implementing a strategy. As most managers would come to learn, paying attention exclusively to the formal structure presented colossal failures in many organizations. The reality of the matter was that by exerting such a one-dimensional focus, managers did not pay attention to other external influences, instead they were consumed on choices based on product or geography. Another negative trait of this approach was its effect on the organization structure as most realignments were implemented briskly and this sudden change in many cases created chaos. Finally, the obsessive focus on structure created stagnation within the organization while the environment was ever changing calling for fresh multidimensional strategies. As such, the notion of structural fit is rarely relied upon and is a dying strategy as most organizations opt for multidimensional flexible strategies in tune with time changes.

3.3 MNC HISTORY & DEFINATION

The first inclines of multinational companies spawned from the vast empires held by Britain, France, Holland and Germany. This period in the 17th and 18th centauries manifested vast British and Dutch companies

An MNC is an entity that has substantial direct investment in foreign countries and actively manages such holdings as an integral part of the company.

3.4 TRADITIONAL MOTIVATIONS FOR MNC's

1. Secure key supplies particularly raw materials such as Aluminum, Copper, Rubber, Oil, etc.
2. Market seeking behavior in order to expand brands to larger markets and exploit economies of scale.
3. Internationalization, acquire low-cost factors of production, capitalize on lower tariffs and government subsidies.

3.5 RISK OF COLLABORATION

Tacit vs. Explicit competences

Given the ever changing and evolving international arena, inherent risks and costs were inevitable. We therefore turn our attention to this very issue of risk and cost. The underlying risk in this situation is the vulnerability one partner may face in terms of their core competences. This situation could take the form where two companies decide to form a strategic alliance in order to compliment skills and resources. Given, these two companies are rival competitors outside this collaboration, the true motives of the parties involved may be to actually gain a competitive edge over the other partner. The potential risk in this collaboration is that one of the partners core competencies and skills could be highly engrained in the larger organizational structure and thus out of reach, where as the other partner's competencies could be explicitly displayed therefore making this partner vulnerable. The greater risk is that once the predatory partner has gained the skills and competencies of the other partner, the collaboration could deteriorate and subsequently collapse as was the situation with the General Foods & Ajinimoto alliance.

Capturing investment initiative

This is also a predatory tactic where the motive is to take advantage of the partnership so as to eliminate the partner's competitive position. In this situation one of the partner's ensures that they are the primary beneficiaries of critical investments by being the aggressor. The danger here lies in the fact that weaker partner could eventually be stripped of its independent decision making thus making it dependant on the aggressive partner.

Costs of collaboration

The biggest and ultimately the most significant cost of a collaboration relate to the opportunity cost the partnership presents to organization as a whole, meaning, are the risks and rewards entailed in the partnership justified and ultimately beneficial to the organization. A comprehensive cost benefit analysis would in part offer an answer to this question. Another inherent cost of collaborations lies in the uncertainties such arrangements present. Since such costs for the most part cannot be predicted or quantified, such uncertainties could present unforeseen additional costs. Internal strife's & conflicts that may result due to the combination of two organizations that have different corporate cultures could create redundancies and unhealthy environment, which in turn creates additional, costs because of inefficiencies within the collaborating structures. Conversely, national background, cultural differences and local political forces often bring about suspicion and in extreme cases resentment of whichever partner is viewed as the outsider, such bias similar to other examples pointed out ultimately is costly to the collaboration in its entirety.

In closing, as we have seen, operating in an international arena presents the MNC management with a very unique set of obstacles and challenges while at the same time offering many potential rewards. The key area the management of an MNC organization needs to focus on is not just a one-dimensional approach but a rather a flexible approach reacting to each situation with a tailor made initiative. The international arena is ever changing and cultural, environmental, and technological factors compound the task. Thus said, an effective MNC manager operating in the international arena has to operate like a fox and pay great emphasis to learning the internal environmental forces at play. Employing a flexible localized organizational structure could have dividends for the organization as well. The international arena is a difficult market but one that not be tamed.

3.6 Copper Mining Operations in Zambia; The Role and Challenges experienced by Multinational Companies

INTRODUCTION

Zambia is a landlocked nation located in central southern Africa, eight countries namely, Tanzania, DRC, Malawi, Namibia, Angola, Mozambique, Botswana and Zimbabwe border it. The land area covers 752,614 square kilometers. The most recent census figures put the population figures at 10 million. The country's GDP was listed at $4.1 billion according to figures from 2003. Zambia has one of the highest urbanized population rates in the Sub-Saharan region with the figure estimated to be at 46%. [1]. The principal city and commercial capital is Lusaka (pop 1.5 million). Other major cities include, Ndola, Kitwe and Livingstone. Copper and Cobalt exports account for 77% of export earnings and the remaining primarily agriculture and tourism. Average daytime temperatures are 15-27 Celsius. Zambia is a country with an enormous amount of mineral resources with copper dominating, other minerals include, zinc, lead nickel, uranium, coal, gemstones, gold, etc. Zambia is however internationally recognized as a major copper and cobalt producer. Since the 1920s when copper production began, the social and economic fabric has heavily relied on this industry.

The primary purpose of this analysis is to explore and examine the copper mining industry in Zambia and how the Multinational Companies have been part of this industry. The case analysis will address some of the strategies employed by the MNCs and point to some successes as well as failures. The opening part of the review presents an overview of the beginning of the copper mining activities in the 1920s Colonial period. The following section looks at the 2nd phase in mining activities, what is described in this review as the post-independence era. The third section examines the decline of the 1970s as world copper prices slumped. Section four gives an incite of the privatization of the Zambian mining industry in the1990s, this section will also give a detailed look at the MNCs that are active players in the privatization efforts. As each chapter unfolds, the review will also look at other pertinent issues. The final segment offers closing remarks and observations.

ZAMBIA COPPER MINING INDUSTRY BACKGROUND

Mining activities in Zambia began in the 1920s in what at the time was called Northern Rhodesia. At that time, the country was under colonial rule under the British government. The British South African Company, a vast conglomerate with mining interests in the African region, first undertook copper exploration and development in the early 1920s spearheaded by Cecil Rhodes who founded the company. [2]. It wasn't until the 1930s that large scale commercialized mining begun. Financing of this operation was undertaken by two of the biggest investors in mining during that period, Alfred Chester Beatty and Ernest Oppenheimer. Chehester Beatty formed the Rhodesian Selection Trust (RST), which was under the control of an American company called American Metal Climax (AMAX) while Ernest Oppenheimer helped create the Rhodesian Anglo-American group of companies. [3].

Mining activities were concentrated in the Northern part of the country, this area would later come to be called the Copperbelt province due to the dominant copper mining activities. The first large-scale commercial mine was Roan Antelope mine opened in 1931 in the town of Luanshya. Nkana mine was the second large-scale mine in Mufulira opened in 1932. Nchanga was opened in 1939. [4]. These three expansive mines would form the basic backbone of the mining sector, the "big 3". Production from the three operations was over 400,000 tones per year and during its peak reached 720,000 tones in 1969 making the Zambia the largest copper producer in the developing world and the world's third largest copper producer behind the United States and the former U.S.S.R. It's copper production accounted for 12.2% of total world production. [5]. This period was the best productive period the Zambian copper industry saw, this early success can be attributed to the high copper prices on the world commodities market. The Zambian economy became a one dimensional economy heavily dependant on foreign exchange derived from copper exports, at the very peak of the copper boom, over 80% of the foreign exchange was from copper export revenues. During this colonial period, British South Africa Company's motive from a global management perspective followed Traditional Motivations, which present companies with "Push and Pull" factors to internationalize. The First recognizable such motivation that drove the company to invest in the Zambian Copper industry relates to the need to secure key supplies, in this case resources. In fact it could be argued that the British South Africa company fits in the mold of early emerging MNCs. Market seeking behavior in this case seems to have played no factor and thus not a motivating pull factor. Availability of lower—cost capital also played no part, no government subsidy enticements were present. Therefore, the motives that were the driving force behind the overseas expansion of the British South African Company into Zambia could be narrowed down to resource seeking behavior. The British South Africa (operating under the two companies mentioned earlier, Rhodesian Selection trust and Rhodesian Anglo—American) company had a significant advantage in its international expansion into Zambia in that the competition aspect was virtually non-existent as it was the pioneering company within this industry and therefore enjoyed exclusive mineral rights with agreements drawn up with the British government. Another advantage the company enjoyed was its experience it had in the mining industry in South Africa, though not particularly in Copper Mining but rather Mining in general, this meant the company had a certain level of existing expertise and competencies engrained within it's organizational framework. This is a very important observation because scholars of transnational management will agree that a company cannot succeed in the international environment unless that company possesses a given set of core competences that allow it to flourish and overcome the barriers the international arena comes with. [6].

The issue of Factor Costs is also worth pointing out, during the colonial era the British Empire was stretching it's reach all across the globe particularly in Africa, Factor Costs clearly played a significant role with the British South Africa Company. Demand for copper was very high in Europe and other parts of the western world but it's availability and ease of access was not readily available and perhaps to some extent not as cost effective, therefore it's abundant availability in Zambia and relatively easy access facilitated the investment decision. We can rule out some of the more recent forces such as global liberal environment, globalization and so forth for obvious reasons i.e., these forces were not on the playing field yet. The British South Africa Company enjoyed enormous success as the paper pointed out earlier, however the fortunes of the British South Africa Company would prove to be short-lived. The early sixties would see a wave of newly emerging independent countries rising from the grips of colonialism, indeed Zambia was not spared from this manifestation and October 24, 1964, the country formally known as Northern Rhodesia formally became an independent sovereign state. Naturally, this new environment had to be somewhat concerning for the British South Africa Company, after all the company had poured substantial capital investments in the Copper Mining industry and it's revenues were at their peek. The tensions and anxieties surrounding the independence movement would pass and operations continued with rising outputs peeking in the late 1960s. However, drastic political economic changes in the early 1970s would change the fortunes of the British South Africa Company when then president Dr Kenneth Kaunda nationalized the mining industry. The industry was consolidated into what was called the Zambia Consolidated Copper Mines Ltd (ZCCM). This effectively ended the era of the British South Africa Company.

POST INDEPENDENCE DECLINING COPPER PRICES

After Zambia became an independent state in 1964, the British government addressed the issue of mineral rights, which up to this point had been exclusively held by the British South Africa Companies. An agreement was reached and the newly formed Zambian government was given the so critical mineral rights. The Zambian government progressively increased their stake into the mining companies and by the early 1970s announced the government's intent to nationalize all critical industries including the mining sector. The government began by purchasing a controlling share into the mining giant MNCs and effectively became the majority owner with 51% ownership. The government would go on to consolidate the copper mining industry into a huge company called the Zambia Consolidated Copper Mines creating one of the largest copper mining companies in the world. [Table 1] This nationalization drive was replicated in all major industries and was not just confined to the mining industry, however the mining industry drew the most attention because of the huge revenues and profits.

Table 1 World's 10 biggest mining companies ('000t)

Rank	Company Name	Production
1.	Codelco (Chile) 1227	
2.	BHP (Australia)	860
3.	Phelps Dodge (USA)	699
4.	Rio Tinto (UK)	648
5.	Freeport (USA)	436
6.	KGHM (Poland)	425
7.	Norilsk (Russia)	360
8.	Cyprus Amax (USA)	341
9.	ZCCM (Zambia)	314
10.	SPCC (USA)	308

Source: Mining Journal, 1997

The Internal political forces within the newly formed country also became interesting as then president Kenneth Kaunda adopted a one-party state with socialist overtures and thus moving away from multi-party democracy. At the same time all these events were unfolding, a new set of external forces were also becoming apparent and these forces would have devastating consequences on the Copper Mining industry in Zambia. World commodity prices for copper, which had always been favorable and consistent began to plunge. The declining global Copper prices inevitably started to be felt at home and the once prosperous mining industry started lagging. Another set back for mining industry was lack of reinvestment in the mining infrastructure which on turn meant plants were deteriorating and production being hampered, in fact production levels dropped from the 600,000 levels down to the 400,000 plus mark. [Table 2.] Even though the Zambia Consolidated Copper Mines was still by far the single largest employer in the country, inefficiencies due to it's large size made it very difficult to efficiently run all the various mining operations and divisions.

Table 2 Exports of Principal Commodities 1965—1993

	Copper	Zinc	Lead	Cobalt	Tobacco
1966	683	45153	15645	1433	9716
1970	684	50334	22079	1814	4041
1975	641	41265	19349	1344	5394
1980	600	30787	8749	1924	1218
1985	474	19024	5122	1924	2604
1990	441	9489	40	4931	2026

Source: Central Statistics Office, Zambia

By the early 90s, twenty years of decline, decay and record low copper prices on the world commodities market had clearly taken its toll on the Zambian copper industry. It was during this period that the political dynamics in Zambia also started taking a different direction. After enduring one-party state politics, voices calling for multi-party democracy were being echoed across the landscape. The political change would eventually be realized as the long time president since independence was defeated in the countries first ever multi-party elections. With the new democratic administration in office, there were renewed calls to resurrect the ailing copper mining industry and bring it back to it's old glory days. These calls would eventually turn to talk of privatizing the entire copper mining industry, the privatization wave was sweeping the whole country with nationalized industries being sold off to private investors but the big question was when and how the mines could be privatized. It was a huge task that would take several years with endless consultations with investors, the World Bank, the IMF and every other conceivable entity. In the mid 1990s, the Zambian government began a full-scale drive to privatize the Zambian Copper mining industry. Bids and tenders were formally put out to the public and major mining companies began to line up and submit bids, the process as one might expect was long and drawn out with a lot of red tape and bureaucracy. In 2000, the Zambian government had completed the comprehensive privatization of the Zambian copper industry. The next section presents an overview of the new companies that entered the Zambian copper industry following privatization.

PRIVATIZATION OF THE ZAMBIAN COPPER INDUSTRY

A.) GLENCORE INTERNATIONAL AG

Glencore is a Swiss company with its primary operational offices in Baar, Switzerland, Stamford, CT, London, England and Singapore. The company has 60 global offices and independent agents in over 50 countries. Its copper mining operations in Zambia began in 2000 and involve a 73% ownership stake in Mopani Copper Mine in the Copperbelt region of Zambia. The mine facility includes 4 underground mines, a concentrator, and cobalt plant with a capacity of 450,000 tons. This is being rebuilt to boost capacity to 650,000 tons [7] the mine facility employs over 7400 employees. Primary export markets are USA, Europe, Asia and the Middle East.

B). Konkola Copper Mines

This is a Zambian registered company with its head office in Chingola, Zambia. 65% of the ownership is by the Zambia Copper Investments Limited of which 51.9% is held by Anglo—American (has since sold controlling interest to Vedanta). The remaining ownership is split between minority stakeholders. The company employs 10,549 employees at its mining operation with over 100 expatriates. The company structure is segmented into five business units or operations listed below:

1. Nchanga—comprised of Nchanga open pit, Nchanga Underground, Nchanga concentrators, Tailings Leach plant & support services.
2. Konkola—Shaft #1, Shaft# 3, Concentrator & support services.
3. Nampundwe—Underground Mine, Concentrator & support services.
4. KCM / Nkana—Smelter, Refinery, Acid Plant & support services.
5. Corporate office

Anglo—America primarily focuses on the smelting, refinery and acid operations. Anglo American has committed $82million in operational costs and contributed an additional $30million in cash. [8]

C). FIRST QUANTUM MINERALS

This is an integrated mining and metals company specializing in copper, cobalt and gold. The company is based in Canada and listed on the Toronto Stock Exchange in Canada. It lists its primary activities as mineral exploration, development and mining. In the Zambian market, it has 100% ownership in the Bwana Mukubwa mine and has an 80% stake ownership in the Kansanshi open pit copper & gold mine. It also has a 16.9% share in the Nkana underground mine as well as 16.9% in the Mufulira mine and smelter operations. The company also holds a18.6% stake in the Australian mining company, Anvil. The company seems well positioned for the Zambian copper industry with its strong diversity strategy.

D.) NFC AFRICA MINING PLC

This is a Chinese company controlled by the Chinese parastatal, China Nonferrous Materials Industry Engineering and Construction Group.) It bought a closed mine from ZCCM in 1998 for $20million and this was followed by repairs and investments of $200 million[9]. The company has an 85% ownership in the Chambeshi mine. The company anticipates production levels of 40,000 to 45,000 ton/year. The company has over 150 Chinese nationals at the facility.

E). AVMIN (ANGLOVAAL MINING LIMITED)

Avmin a South African mining company got into the industry with two ventures. The first venture was an 80% stake in the Konkola North project while the second venture was a 90% stake in the Chanbeshi cobalt plant. Avmin presents an interesting case study, because it entered the market with very ambitious objectives and pumped a reported $100million in the investments[10]. Despite these huge investments and commitments, Avmin would later announce that it was disinvesting and getting out of the Zambian copper industry due to overwhelming constraints and failing to break even.

F). OTHER NOTABLE PLAYERS

1. BINANI GROUP—Indian company with 85% ownership in Luanshya underground mine.
2. VANTAGE ENTERPRISES CORP—Canadian company involved mainly in Amethyst gemstones.
3. Cyprus Amax Kansanshi plc—U.S. Company with 80% stake in Kansanshi mine
4. Phelps Dodge corp.—U.S. Company, 100% stake in Lumwana deposit.
5. Adastra Minerals—Canadian company involved in exploratory ventures.
6. Quasim Mining(Colossal recourses corp.)—Canadian company, 60% of Kabwe cobalt trails.

CONCLUDING REMARKS

The Zambian copper industry seems to have gone full circle, from the early discoveries and commercial production of copper deposits by the pioneering Cecil Rhodes, the British South Africa Company involvement, the nationalization efforts post independence and ironically back to what is seemingly like the starting point, copper production back in the private sector. One thing is clear, the nationalization efforts with seeming good intentions of self—sufficiency were perhaps too bold and flawed from the onset. To begin with, the Zambian government lacked the foresight to consider just how important the expertise to run such large—scale operations entailed. Secondly, the government run nationalized company had so many inefficiencies and overlooked reinvestment back into the operations and thus the facilities continued to deteriorate and produce below par. Given the low commodity copper prices were depressed, the production levels could still have been better. The new privatization quest is a very positive step in resurrecting this industry, the vibrant environment within the industry and the large capital investments by international companies is already paying dividends as not only are production levels rising, but more importantly, the world copper market price is slowly climbing as well. There is a glimmer of hope and I anticipate a very positive outcome for the Zambian copper industry and economy overall

REFERENCE NOTES

1. http://usembassy.state.gov/zambia/cguide.html
2. United Nations Environment Programme report by Grijp,Nicoliene;
1 Mupimpila,Christoper. pg15
2 http://www.iisd.org/susprod/copper.pdf#search='copper%20mining%20in%20zambia'
3. United Nations Environment Programme report by Grijp,Nicoliene;
   Mupimpila,Christoper.
   http://www.iisd.org/susprod/copper.pdf#search='copper%20mining%20in%20zambia'
4. www.zambiamining.com
5. Bostock & Harvey, 1972
6. Bartlett,Birkinshaw, Ghoshal, S. 2004 Transnational Management. Pg7
7. www.glencore.com
8. Anglo American Fact Sheet
9. US Geological Society
10. www.mining.co.za/copperbelt
    Table 2: Mining Journal, 1997

3.7 Case Analysis: Pilgrims Pride Corporation
Current Stated Mission
- Provide outstanding customer satisfaction every day.

Objectives
- Double in size every five to ten years through international growth and acquisitions.
- Become major player in food service market
- Improve margins and stock performance
- Dominate Mexican market

Objectives and Strategies employed

Double in size: in order to achieve this goal, pilgrim's pride is intent on horizontall integrations and acquisitions of competitor companies in the chicken industry as shown by its two most recent acquisitions in 2000 and 2003 of WLR Foods, Inc., and ConAgra. The company utilizes a horizontal integration strategy. The company also seeks to continue expanding its dominant Mexican presence relying on its name recognition within that market, pilgrims pride thus employees a market penetration strategy to promote and reinforce its widely recognized name brand in Mexico.

Become major player in the food service market: in order to achieve this goal, pilgrims positioned its self as an alternative to Tyson, it's primary competitor and also relied on a massive advertising campaign costing $6—$8 million a year. The company used a market penetration strategy in seeking increased market share through its advertising marketing campaign.

Improve margins and Stock performance: pilgrims relies on its horizontal integrations & acquisitions, through such integrations, it hopes to capitalize on the synergistic benefits and therefore improving its overall bottom line. The strategy followed is a horizontal integration strategy

Dominate Mexican market: has it's plants located to serve over 85 percent of the Mexican market in order to reach its goal of becoming the most efficient operator in Mexico. The company utilizes market penetration and horizontal strategies.

Pilgrims strengths, weaknesses, opportunities and threats.

Internal Strengths

A). Pilgrims has attained a house hold name brand recognition and this has allowed it to compete as an alternative to the industry leader Tyson as represented with the U.S. poultry production numbers, 23 percent (Tyson) and 16 percent (Pilgrims).

B). One of the key strengths for pilgrims lies in its strong presence in the Mexican market and its strategically located plants that carter over 85 percent of the Mexican market. The importance of this factor is exemplified by pilgrims sales numbers in Mexico, $228 million in 1996 and $343 million in 2002 representing a 50 percent increase.

C). Pilgrims boasts a better employee retention record than the industry, its turnover rate at 16 percent is far better than the industry average of 60 percent.

D). Pilgrims acquisitions have enabled it to have a growth rate of 9.7 percent compared to the industry rate of 4.5 percent.

E). Strong sales particularly in further processed chicken with increases of over 50 percent between 1998 through 2002.

Internal Weaknesses

A). Management has not diversified into other food products such as beef or pork, relies too much on poultry which is very has great price vitality.

B). Plant health concerns as evidenced by the 2002 largest food recall in USDA. history involving 27million pounds of chicken from the WLR facility.

External Opportunities

A). Chicken per capita consumption has been constantly rising with the USDA estimating a continued 3% future annual growth rate, this resulting growth presents an opportunity for offering new products.

B). Consumption rates for chicken products overseas as well have increased and these markets are underserved which is a great opportunity for exports of value added products and low value products as well.

C). Changing population and demographic variables mean people more often than ever are on the go, this resulting fast pace lifestyle creates an opportunity for quick pre-packaged meals, a great opportunity for pilgrims to introduce new value added products.

D). Increased income and wealth levels have meant people are more apt eat out or order than cooking at home which in turn is another excellent opportunity for new product development.

E). Health conscious consumers concerned about nutritional facts opting for white meat rather than red meat, this is a growing segment which can be further capitalized.

F). Price of chicken cheaper than red meat.

External Threats

A). Labor recruitment and retention is a big concern, this type of business involves very grueling and undesirable working conditions with minimal pay therefore making it very difficult to fill or keep jobs. Labor shortages a great concern.

B). Salmonella and bacterial outbreaks in chicken factories pose a threat that result in expensive recalls.

C). Legal actions from Animal rights groups such as PETA

D). Takeover bid by primary competitor, Tyson.

E). Safety concerns in production facilities, numbers by the Occupational Safety and Health Administration in 2000 reveal one in seven poultry workers sustained injuries on the job, such seeming high numbers could spun a class action lawsuit.

Pilgrims SWOT table

	STRENGTHS - S	WEAKNESSES - W
	1. Strong brand name 2. Dominant Mexican market 3. Better employment retention than industry 4. Remarkable growth & acquisitions 5. Continued strong sales	1. Not diversified in beef & pork market 2. Plant health concerns 3. Pending litigation
OPPORTUNITIES - O 1. Surging chicken consumption numbers 2. Value added products 3. Changing demographic behaviors, more demand for pre-packaged meals 4. International market increased demand 5. Health conscious public	**SO STRATEGIES** 1. Add new value added products and strongly push these products using brand name. 2 Use experience from Mexican market presence to enter new international markets 3. Use strong brand targeting growing health conscious population.	**WO STRATEGIES** 1. Create new value added products 2. Enhance export of non value products to international markets
THREATS - T 1. Labor shortages 2. Animal Rights groups 3. Health & working conditions litigations 4. Take over by Tyson	**ST STRATEGIES** 1. Enhance what has made them better than the industry average in employment retention, and use this as a recruiting tool.	**WT STRATEGIES** 1. Enhance plant health and safety procedures and put in place more safety officers

External Audit

External Factor Evaluation for Pilgrims Pride Corporation

KEY ETERNAL FACTORS (WT,RATING,WT SCORE)

Opportunities

1. Chicken per capita consumption has been increasing, at 78 pounds, the USDA estimates 3% yearly growth.(0.20 WT, 4 Rating, 0.80 Wt Score)
2. Per capita consumption in Mexico, up from about 30-50 pounds (0.20 WT 4Rating, 0.80 WT Score)
3. Changing population dynamics, more mobile and affluent (0.15Wt, 2 Rating 0.30 WT Score)
4. Health conscious consumers(0.05 WT, 1 Rating, 0.05 WT Score)
5. Chicken cheaper than red meat (0.05WT, 1 Rating, 0.05 WT Score)

Threats

1. Labor retention and recruitment difficult. (0.05 WT, 4 Rating, 0.20 WT Score)
2. Salmonella & Bacterial spread in processing plants (0.10WT,1 Rating, 0.10 WT Score).
3. Legal actions from Animal rights groups such as PETA. (0.05WT, 2 Rating, 0.10WT Score)
4. Takeover bid by primary competitor Tyson. (0.05WT, 2 Rating, 0.10 WT Score).
5. Safety concerns in production facilities, (0.10 WT, 2 Rating, 0.20WT Score)

*Note that WT x Rating = WT Score)

Total WT = 1.00

Total WT Score = 2.70

2.70 weight is an above average response to external environmental forces

Internal Audit

IFE Matrix for Pilgrims Pride Corporation

KEY INTERNAL FACTORS (WT,RATING, WT SCORE)

Strengths

1. Pilgrims has attained a house hold name brand recognition. (0.10, 3, 0.30)
2. Strong presence in the Mexican market and its strategically located plants that carter over 85 percent of the Mexican market (0.20, 4, 0.80)
3. Pilgrims boasts a better employee retention record than the industry. (0.05, 4, 0.20)
4. Pilgrims acquisitions have enabled it to have a growth rate of 9.7 percent compared to the industry rate of 4.5 percent.(0.15, 4, 0.60)
5. Strong sales particularly in further processed chicken with increases of over 50 percent between 1998 through 2002. (0.15, 4,0.60).

Weaknesses

1. Management has not diversified into other food products such as beef or pork. (0.10,1, 0.10)
2. Plant health concerns as evidenced by the 2002 largest food recall in USDA history. (0.15,2, 0.30)
3. Plant working conditions. (0.10,2,0.20)
   TOTAL WT Score = 3.10
   3.10 score well above average.

Pilgrims Prides position on the Grand Strategy Matrix

Pilgrims Pride appears to be located in Quadrant 1, it is in excellent strategic position and overwhelmingly concerned with market penetration and market development.

1. Market development: as shown by its entry into overseas markets
2. Market penetration: exhibited by continued growth
3. Product development: is engaged in developing new value added products
4. Forward integration: exhibits some regional control over distributors
5. Backward integration: has control over supplier/poultry farmers through contracting arrangements

6. Horizontal integration: pilgrim has been involved in key competitor acquisitions

7. Concentric diversification: introduction of various value added products.

Revised Mission and Objectives

After careful consideration, the current stated mission "Provide outstanding customer satisfaction every day" while good, clear and concise, the direction of this company and for strategic reasons, I feel the Bo Pilgrim's personal mission is more in concert with the vision and more importantly follows with the company's strong presence in the Mexican market. This mission would also further enhance Pilgrims name brand recognition and allegiance in the Mexican market. Emphasizing American and Mexican jobs creates an instant bonding effect with customers in the U.S. and Mexico, in turn a win-win situation. I also feel the primary objective (dominating the Mexican market) is well echoed in this statement and the 9 components of a mission statement are captured, thus said my revised mission is that of Bo Pilgrim:

· "The mission behind Pilgrim's is to help save rural America in the United States and the people of Mexico by providing jobs in the production of chickens. They must be versatile, economical, and wholesome chickens to feed the rest of the world. We'll use the best affordable technology and science to improve our systems. That's broader than just making money out of chickens."

The objectives are intact and I see no need for revision, my observation would suggest that the quest to dominate the Mexican market needs to be isolated as the single most important goal because this a high growth market and pilgrim is in an excellent position to dominate this market. Its production facilities are strategically located to access over 85% of this market, the goal needs to be 100% access. The Mexican market is of significant importance because of the growth and the sales already generated by Pilgrim, over $300 million in 2002, a 50% leap from 1996. Another key recommendation would be for Pilgrim's to produce value added products specifically designed to carter to the Mexican market and cultural taste preferences, the company would then use market penetration, product development and market development strategies.

Implementation of new strategy

International Management, R& D and Marketing

The international management team needs to have a clear understanding of what is expected of them in implementing a new value added product designed for the Mexican market, therefore it is critical for communication channels between the headquarters in Texas to be clear, concise and understandable to the overseas management team in Mexico. This requires a direct supervision and overall control of a divisional president/CEO stationed in Mexico who can see the day to day implementation of product development This divisional head would in turn work directly with project managers from the Marketing, R & D, Human Resource and Finance departments. There also needs to be special cultural considerations that may appear okay domestically but carry different connotations with the Mexican culture. The international management team will be tasked with setting budgetary parameters, local promotion campaigns and researching local legal laws for successful implementation. The international management team will work very closely with the R& D team to make sure product development is within budgetary allocation and is implemented on a timely fashion to allow for the marketing department to appropriately launch a promotional campaign. The marketing department will be delegated for test marketing and overall promotion & marketing. All channels will be utilized, i.e., print media, radio, television, internet and so forth.

Human Resource

The human resource department will be responsible for recruiting talented experts with an understanding of the Mexican chicken product market in order to facilitate a niche opening for new value added products. The human resource team will also be responsible for training, support functions, and managing a diverse workforce.

Evaluation

The following timetable would be used to measure effectiveness of strategy

Step1.

R&D intensive Mexican market research for feasibility of new value added product. 1-2years

Step 2

Test marketing by marketing department 6 months to 12 months

Step 3

Limited Trial launch (3 months)

Step 4

Full Launch or Abort product launch contingent on step 3 outcome.

CHAPTER IV
U.S. Labor Law Relations

Thehe student will find material presented in this section of a survey nature designed to familiarize the student with the various methods and techniques involved in collective bargaining both in the private and public sector. In addition, a brief sweep of the statutory, administrative and case law in American Labor Law are discussed.

The overall objective for the student is to develop a basic understanding of labor relation's terms, practices and law. However this should not limit the student as other key specific objectives can also be attained, these include:

1. Demonstrate knowledge of labor relations terms, practices and law.
2. Apply that knowledge in the context of various real life circumstances
3. Analyze contemporary labor relation issues utilizing concepts developed during the reading
4. Utilize material from this section as a foundation for preparation to a professional career.

4.1 Early Developments in Labor Law
a) Conspiracy Theory

The Conspiracy Theory was borne in the early 1800's as a tool by employer's to curb the activities of shoemaker unions. Employing this doctrine, employers utilized the court's to enforce the law on guilty conspirators, by subjecting violator's with imprisonment and fines. The stem of the theory lies in determining harm by a group of two or more people inflicted on other people or society as a whole. To support this theory, employers urged that unions by the very nature of their activities raised wages thereby harming the general public. They further argued that the resulting wage manipulation by union activity was unnatural and therefore taking advantage of the public. The resulting wage increases were also said to be responsible for higher prices of commodities, which in turn created greater harm to productivity as a whole, caused unemployment, damaged trade and ultimately infringed on the rights of all worker's.

Current Applicability of conspiracy theory

Conditions to allow for this theory are as follows,

- There has to be an agreement of two or more parties engaged in illegal means.
- The second condition stipulates, conspirator's can be punished for acts even if acting in a co-conspirator role.

b) Injunctions

The widespread use of injunctions as relates to early union activities can be attributed to two primary factors. The first being the 1895 US Supreme court ruling that upheld the injunction as a constitutional tool to stop union activities (Deb's case). The second factor argued that injunctions could be used to protect property against irreparable damage. The damage to property notion was widely used to include an array of union activities, which were viewed as a hindrance to free access of the labor pool and market's therefore constituting damage to property. To a large extent, the failure & decline of the conspiracy theory contributed to the labor injunction, as the conspiracy theory became less effective, employer's felt they needed a more effective tool to curb worker's engaged in union activity. In addition, employer's realized conspiracy trials were long, complicated, cumbersome and took too long to resolve, thus the birth of the labor injunction.

Unlike its predecessor, the labor injunction proved to be quick, simple and precise. Injunctions are issued by Judges in absence of juries and once issued must be obeyed immediately. They come in three forms:

i) temp. restraining order

ii) temp. injunction

iii) permanent injunction

The popularity of injunctions brought about a tremendous amount of abuses. Some of the more common abuses included the indiscriminant manner by which judges employed this tool under the umbrella of damage to property. Other issues that arose as a result of injunctions included the notion of judges also acting as legislators.

Current Applicability: All three types are used today in both labor and non—labor cases.

c) Yellow Dog Contracts

This is a tool that was employed by antiunion employers to eliminate the union movement. The principle trait of this tool was the promise made to prospective employees during the hiring promise not to engage in union activity. The widespread use of this tool was further enhanced by the passage of the Hitchman-Decision that upheld the use of labor injunctions to enforce yellow—dog contracts.

Current Applicability: Yellow Dog contracts were made illegal with the passage of the Norris-La Guardia Act, this legislation effectively voided the Hitchman decision. The Norris La Guardia Act denied courts the authority to enforce yellow dog contract's pointing out the conflict of interest. Subsequently, the NLRB would state that employer's attempting yellow dog tactics were engaging in unfair labor practices. It is important to note that yellow dog contracts were in use for 15yrs plus.

d) Antitrust Statutes

These statutes were passed by congress to protect unions from being prosecuted. The Norris—La Guardia Act with its antitrust laws shielded unions, which was not the case with the Clayton Act. The Norris La Guardia Act was also a message the Supreme Court stated in reaction to the Bedford Cut Stone case.

Current Applicability: Unions still protected from prosecution by antitrust statutes as long as they do not hamper trade.

4.2 Procedure for filing an Unfair Labor Practice Complaint

Unfair Labor Practices Procedures:

Step 1. Formal charge initiated (Parties fail to reach compromise)

Step 2. Investigation (Field examination conducted)

Step 3. Regional Director complaint (at this level, the following 3 outcomes can derail charge):

A) Withdrawal—case can be withdrawn

B) Settlement—settlement can be reached between parties

C) No Merit—case could be disposed as having no merit to advance

* if case is derailed by any one of these factors, appeal could be made to General Counsel whose decision is final and non-review able.

Step 4. Hearing (presided by administrative law judge)

Step 5. NLRB (20 day window to appeal)

Step 6. Court of Appeals (if warranted)

Step 7. Supreme court (if warranted).

4.3 NLRB (National Labor Relations Board) Jurisdiction

The Wagner Act provided the NLRB authority to have jurisdiction over unfair labor practices and other arising questions related to interstate commerce. Due to the broad mandate offered to the NLRB, the Supreme Court allows for congress to play a role in certain matters. The NLRB essentially operates at its discretion regarding which cases to pursue and in what manner to operate. Given such a broad mandate resulted in some complications for the board. One such problem in the NLRB earlier days was that of case selection due to the heavy workloads and budget constraints, the board would overlook cases that tended to have minimal impact on commerce and invariably took up cases where the impact to commerce was substantial. Another concern relating to jurisdiction was the issue of federal v. state jurisdiction, the Wagner Act and Taft—Hartley amendments sought to clearly define the role and jurisdiction of the NLRB, most issues relating unfair labor practices were deferred to the NLRB with the federal courts available for ultimate decisions if warranted. Another product of these amendments was the establishment of uniform application of NLRB policy. Landrum—Griffin: title vii addressed the issue of "no man's land" in response to the cases not picked up by the NLRB being left in void as states would not deal with them.

Under the NLRA, public employees at federal, state & local levels are excluded, others include federal contractors, domestic servants, agriculture workers, etc. Some notable expansions of groups covered by the board include, sports professional teams, private colleges/universities, charitable institutions, undocumented aliens etc..

The NLRB has not fully exercised its potential jurisdiction in a variety of fashions. The primary failure lies in the beauracratic delay in resolving cases. Another source of failure relates to fact that the NLRB may only hear cases referred to it by the general counsel, thereby making the board somewhat weak. The board also has no recourse in challenging cases derailed by the general counsel. The changing make up of NLRB board members also results in constant shifting views.

The role of states in labor relations seems uncertain and hazy; the issue of "no man's land " seems particularly disturbing. Supreme court decisions take an unfavorable view over state mandate in labor disputes, which leaves states with an undefined role in labor relations.

4.4 Collective Bargaining

Are Plant (Factory) employees included as a single collective bargaining unit?

The NLRB determines whether all employees of a plant are to be included as a single bargaining unit on a case-by-case basis. Each defined group of worker's is examined in view of the circumstances at play, below is a synopsis of each group:

Craft workers essentially are considered on a case-by-case basis. Current policy follows the "Mallinckrodt Doctrine" Board outlined six basic guidelines:

1. Status of employees
2. Existing bargaining trends
3. Distinctive identities of general workforce
4. Bargaining history in industry
5. Integration & interdependency
6. Qualification & experience of union

Supervisors may organize but have no protection

Managers are excluded from being part of a single collective bargaining unit, this policy is as a result of the Supreme Court ruling in the Bell Aerospace case, which stated managers not covered by law.

Plant guards may not be part of a single collective bargaining unit as stipulated in Taft-Hartley, they may however bargain with fellow guards but are prohibited from organizing with other workers. In order for professionals to be part of a collective bargaining unit, the board has to allow these employees to vote in a special election. Confidential employees are excluded.

Procedure for processing representation elections

Step 1. Petition (recognition)

Step 2. Investigation conducted

Step 3. Regional Director level (could issue withdrawal or stipulated election at this stage)

Step 4. Hearing (by field examiner)

*Can be appealed after this stage before decision

Step 5. Certify/decertify/no cert (Regional director)

Step 6. NLRB need not review

Step 7. Court of appeals (if warranted)

Step 7. Supreme court (if warranted)

4.5 Explaining the "General Shoe Doctrine"

NLRB can reject or place aside election results in the absence of unfair labor practices if it deems either party involved have engaged in behavior capable of swaying employees from making a free choice during an election. The pivotal aspect of this doctrine focuses on the impediment of an atmosphere conducive to free choice during an election. Behavior such as visiting employees at their homes and presuring them to reject the union or a manager conspiring with employees in his/her office to shoot down the union is certain to have the NLRB apply the Shoe Doctrine. In applying the shoe doctrine, the board conducts a thorough investigation of the circumstances at play.

Employer Do's and Don'ts in interfering with employees

An employer may:

1.) Call a captive audience staff meeting for all employees without affording the union equal time to reply.

2.) Make economic predictions based on a factual basis of what the believe will be the resulting effects of unionization, in making such predictions, the employer needs to be cautious from making suggestive innuendos bashing unions.

3.) An employer also has a lawful right to express their opinions provided no threats or coercion are part of such opinions.

An employer may not:

1.) Make threats to employees

2.) Assert coercion tactics

3.) Make promises to sway employees voting decision

4.) Visit employee homes for purpose discouraging them from voting for union

5.) Lie or Misrepresent facts

6.) Single out or harass employees

When can an employer petition the NLRB to conduct an election?

The Taft-Hartley legislation allows an employer to petition the board for new elections in the event the employer is confronted with two unions both looking for recognition within the same bargaining unit. This stipulation allows the employer to petition for elections even if only one of the two unions is demanding overall collective bargaining. Recognition status of the union has to exist before an employer can proceed with such a petition. Once a petition is filed, the board conducts a careful investigation of all factors prior to making a final determination.

Gissell Doctrine Explained

Under this doctrine, the NLRB can give unions bargaining recognition even if the union loses representation elections provided there is existing evidence of an employer practicing unfair labor practices during an election campaign. The logic of this doctrine follows that by allowing a new election in light of unfair labor practices carried out, employees are likely to follow the same voting pattern given another opportunity. Majority support for the union as a bargaining representative prior to the election has to evidenced in the form of signed authorization cards (75% practical). Two conditions exist for unions to obtain certification without an election:

1.) **Jay silk type**—unfair labor practices taking place & employer refusing to allow employer requests to bargain, no election held, union must show majority cards.

2.) **Bernel foam type**—similar to above except election held.

Types of Gissell Doctrines

A.) Atrocious/pervasive—can issue bargaining order regardless of election or majority status.

B.) Serious—UFLP, requires evidence of card majority.

C.) Minor—minimal impact, no bargaining order, but general shoe applies.

A seemingly reasonable policy because in its absence, unethical employers could continue to curtail employee's freedom of choice by continuously using unfair labor practices such as threats and coercion. Without measures to stop or discourage such practices, you end with situations like sweatshops or certain third world nations where employee's rights are non—existent. It is only fair that employers obey the law therefore avoid being caught up in such a predicament.

Issue of Closed Shops and right to work states

Unions and employers may not negotiate for the closed shop. The closed shop was outlawed by congress through the passage of the Taft—Hartley legislation. Unions and employers in some states may negotiate for a union shop, this is contingent on each individual state and it's stance on union shops. They may not negotiate for union shops in right to work states as this practice of union shops has been eliminated under their state legislation. Such states have statutes within their constitutions that ban the pre-requisite union membership as a condition for employment.

4.6 Successor Employer Obligations

The U.S. Supreme Court decision in "Burns Protective Agency" is still the legal binding framework for employers in matters relating to the successor employer. The Burns decision stipulates a successor employer must recognize a predecessor's bargaining unit, but is not obligated to accept the labor agreement negotiated with the previous employer. This decision was further enhanced in 1987 when the U.S. Supreme Court upheld the NLRB use of the "Burns" doctrine. The U.S. Supreme Court was careful in pointing out that the NLRB and the courts deal with Successor problems on a case-by-case basis.

In summary, the criteria in successor employer issues is as follows:

1. An employer is required to recognize a predecessor union and has duty to bargain if the

Conditions below are satisfied.

A). Company retains the same structure

B). The majority of old employees are hired or retained. (Note, if the successor employer is

in doubt of this stipulation, the employer may raise a good faith doubt, however

They need to present object evidence supporting their doubts).

2. A successor employer is not required to abide by the prior bargaining agreement.

4.7 Reinstatement rights in varying circumstances

The issue of reinstatement rights of strikers varies depending on the nature of the strike, before further discussing this issue; a brief synopsis of each type of strike is essential.

Economic Strike: encompasses strikes that typically call for higher wages, call for better working conditions, working hour issues, better benefits etc.

Unfair Labor Practice Strike: this is a strike that results from an employer deemed to be engaging in conduct declared unlawful by the NLRB policy. Usually involves things such as union recognition matters, impediment of the collective bargaining process, employer interference in union organization or elections, and so forth.

Jurisdiction Strike: relates to dispute between two or more unions over the delegation of work assignments. (Illegal under Taft—Hartley)

Other types include:

Wildcat strikes

Certification/minority strikes

Sympathy strikes.

Reinstatement under Economic Strikes

Employees engaging in economic strikes have very limited rights in terms of reinstatement. Such employees are not required to be reinstated and may be permanently replaced, unless employer engages in unfair labor practices in the process. The NLRB may order immediate reinstatement of such workers only if the employer does not fill their jobs with permanent replacements. The legal stance of employers being able to replace economic strikers with permanent replacements was borne out of the U.S supreme court ruling in NLRB v. Mackay Radio & Telegraph. The courts further revisited this matter in 1986 where it reaffirmed its initial position. An employer is not required to reinstate economic strikers and may permanently replace economic strikers unless there is evidence of unfair labor practice.

Right to vote unless:

1.) Find new permanent job

2.) Job has been eliminated

3.) Evidence of misconduct.

Reinstatement under Unfair Labor Strike

Employees that fall into this category have unlimited rights regarding reinstatement, striking workers are required to be reinstated regardless of whether an employer has replaced them. The NLRB has the overwhelming mandate not only to order reinstatement but may also instruct the employer to pay back wages & other lost benefits. Notable cases asserting this position include the Mastro Plastics case where the U.S. supreme court held that employees were entitled to reinstatement even if the strike was in violation of the no-strike clause in a labor agreement, contingent on the strike having stemmed from employer unfair labor practice conduct. One important aspect to note is the forfeiture of reinstatement rights if any violence is involved.

Reinstatement under Jurisdiction Strikes

As earlier pointed out, such strikes are illegal as stipulated in Taft—

Hartley. When jurisdiction disputes arise, the NLRB (as instructed in the 1961 U.S. supreme court case of Columbia Broadcasting System) is to hear arguments presented by both parties involved and make a decision, provided the parties involved have not established a mechanism to resolve such issues within 10 days. In 1971, the U.S. Supreme Court under "Plasterers Local 79" clarified its stand giving the NLRB mandate to settle jurisdictional disputes if the employer refuses or fails to submit dispute to an outside party for a resolution.

Reinstatement under Recognition Strikes

Sometimes referred to as strikes against certifications or minority strikes. Congress outlawed such strikes for recognition when there is an existing NLRB certified union. Anyone engaging in such a strike where a certified NLRB union is present in essence is practicing an unfair labor practice as defined in section 8(b). If such a strike proceeds, the NLRB under section 10(1) is given authority to seek injunctions against strikers. In summation, recognition strikes are:

- Illegal
- No reinstatement
- No Voting.

Unions and Hand billing Practices

A Union may use such a tactic as long as they are not physically harassing consumers or causing disruptions such as blocking traffic, or any other acts constituting disorderly conduct. This issue was bought to the forefront in the 1998 case involving the De Bartolo Corporation at one of its shopping malls in Tampa, Florida. The U.S. Supreme Court unanimously voted that the practice of hand billing was lawful, effectively reversing the earlier position taken by the NLRB. The court stated unions could handbill a shopping mall in order to try to get the owner to unionized workers.

Control mechanisms regarding dues etc

As regards dues, initiation fees and assessments, different requirements apply based upon the type of union. Local unions can raise dues, initiation fees or assessments via secret ballots in two ways listed below:

1.) Vote taken at membership meeting with a reasonable notice having been allowed detailing that the issue will be put forward to members for a vote .

2.) Membership referendum, posted notices as well as announcements may be utilized to satisfy the reasonable notice requirement.

National Unions follow the criteria outlined below:

1.) Majority of delegates at regular convention (delegates selected by secret vote plus 30 days notice)

2.) Majority, secret vote by referendum

3.) Majority of vote of executive board if given authority in by— laws

Fiduciary Responsibility:

- Loans to members limited
- May not pay fines for unlawful conduct of officials.

Due process protections for Union members regarding disciplinary action

Union members may not be fined , expelled, or disciplined without due process protocol being followed. Landrum-Griffin in it's "bill of rights" outlined the following procedures to be followed when union are to be reprimanded.

A.) Union member must be served in writing with specific charges.

B.) Union member should be given reasonable time to prepare their defense.

C.) Member should be given a full and fair hearing.

If a union violates any of these procedural standards, the union member in question has the right to initiate a court challenge of the action levied. The U.S. Supreme Court made it clear that the courts in such matters were limited to procedural determinations and not to be embroiled in specific union rules[1971 ruling & 1992 Chicago Federal appeals court case]. The burden of enforcement of the purported violations of bill of rights is placed upon the union member suing unions or it's officers in civil court.

Discrimination based on sex, race or religion

The passage of Title VII made it illegal for an employer as well as unions to discriminate based on sex, race, religion, disability or age. Congress formed the Equal Employment Opportunity Commission to administer the broad legislation. Clearly, the legal framework is in place to deal with discriminatory issues, however it is notable to address some oddities. The first issue pertains to sexual orientation, such preferences are not governed by any federal statues but rather left to the state statutes. The second odd exception involves the notion of BFOQ where out of business necessity, the employee make up is comprised of a certain gender, the business necessity is job related and carries non-discriminatory intent or consequence.

Should Federal employees be allowed to collectively bargain?

Federal employees should be allowed to engage in collective bargaining as long as their position does not compromise national security or civil law & order. By allowing bargaining in the federal realms, this would not only satisfy the wishes of those federal employees who desire to do so but may also force some government agencies in being run more efficiently as they realize that they are being held to the same standards as the private sector in employee related matters. The critical issue goes back to maintaining a balance between protecting the greater good of society or allowing for bargaining to satisfy federal employees who may desire bargaining, until that balance is quantifiable in terms of opportunity cost, the logistics are still gray.

Current labor law—pro labor or pro employer?

The current labor law status has come a long way, and through it's journey has bestowed a great deal of progress to worker rights. However, the current environment seems rather edged towards the employer, not necessarily by design in my viewpoint but rather as a result of changing times and the free—market system at hand. The changing climate of labor law can be seen in the rising number of work free states particularly the Sun Belt states where their state statutes are overwhelmingly pro-business. I honestly see this trend intensifying and spreading as the success in some of these pro-business states begin to manifest themselves. My answer is not solely as a result of the declining membership numbers of NLRB even though that in itself gives credence to my observation. I do not think this trend, i.e. pro-business environment is such a bad thing, and I think it will take a while for society to adjust their skills to cope with this new order of business.

4.8 THE DEMISE OF U.S. UNIONS IN THE GLOBALIZATION ERA:

VICTIM OR CORPORATE IRRESPONSIBILITY?

The U.S. labor movement has undoubtedly had a tremendous impact on labor relations over decades acting as a voice and guardian for worker's rights. Along the way, the labor movement has confronted obstacles from employer's and other anti-union forces but always exhibited a tenacity to forge ahead in achieving its goals. Despite various pitfalls and sustained criticism of the movement, many positives for workers have resulted due to the labor campaign, one need only look at the various legislations and amendments passed over the years ensuring the protection of workers rights. Unions today and for a while as a matter of fact are at a pivotal crossroad, their membership numbers have dwindled to all time lows, collective bargaining has been marginalized, and most troubling for the labor movement is the continued erosion of union jobs as they are relocated elsewhere. The relocation of production facilities and the shift in the workforce is the cornerstone of this paper. The subject of globalization is obviously very extensive and all encompassing, thus this case study will focus on two specific subject matters as relates to the globalization environment. The first part of the case review lays emphasis on the mobility of production facilities and the latter part of the review examines the dilemma of the changing workforce immigrant conducive states. In each case, I will examine the scope and nature of the issue from the perspective of unions and employers. Applicable law, if any will be addressed as well as other factors at play. Naturally, both parties, that is unions and employers have varying views on this subject matter, which will be addressed, in the latter part of this review.

LABOR & EMPLOYER RELATIONS OVERVIEW

A brief perspective of labor relations and unions is essential in setting the stage for the issues at hand. The development of labor relations is an interesting journey dating back to the pre 1930's to its current state. This relationship has evolved with times and undergone a variety of changes. The first part of the relationship saw a dominant judicial system playing a heavy hand in regulation.[1]. Unionism saw it's rise in the 1930's with it's membership reaching astonishing numbers, this dramatic rise was fostered by the passage of the Norris—La Guardia and Wagner legislation which promoted unionism and collective bargaining.[2] During this period, federal and state courts made it difficult and in some cases impossible to form unions. Prior to the Norris—La Guardia era, the environment for the labor movement was very hostile and unpleasant, employers utilized tactics such as the "conspiracy theory", injunctions, yellow-dog contracts, and so forth. Such tactics ran out of steam and simply faded away with time or were nullified by Norris—La Guardia as was the case with Yellow—Dog contracts. The Wagner act under section 8(a)(1) made it an unfair labor practice for an employer to use tactics that undermined employee's rights [3]. As such, the Wagner act provided the NLRB authority to have jurisdiction over unfair labor practices and other arising questions involving interstate commerce.

The current environment enjoys an array of legal protection for workers, however the dynamic is constantly evolving and changing . Unions today are faced with new challenges under the global environment, unlike some of the earlier battles waged on home turf, unions now have to contend with crafty employers who have found a new weapon in their arsenal. Where as unions had relied on collective bargaining and strikes as negotiating tools with employers, such tools have been marginalized by employers as they simply move their production facilities elsewhere to avoid dealing with unions. Employers are also effectively using loopholes in shifting traditional workforce patterns. As earlier pointed out, unions by their very nature are and have always been a very tenacious group which has put up a commendable fight over the years, however, this fight with globalization is daunting &perhaps their biggest , the very survival of unions may come down to this battle ground. The labor movement has taken some heavy blows from the manifestations of globalization and they will need all the muscle they can garner for this battle.

MOBILITY OF PRODUCTION FACILITIES

This is perhaps one of the biggest threats looming on the very existence of American unions as we know them. The continued relocation of American production facilities to various locales across the globe which in most cases are developing countries has reached epic proportions. Ironically, the very basic rights unions evolved out of, i.e., fighting for employee rights is at the pinnacle of this trend. The very lack of such employee rights in developing countries is actually fostering this movement. Since labor costs are significantly much lower in such developing nations, compounded with the absence of enforceable labor protection laws & other factors such as corruption, poverty etc, the rapid disappearance of union jobs has continued. As this trend has steadily risen, the effect on American jobs lost is astounding; "between 1969 to 1976, 1.2 million jobs lost, 1980 to 1985, 2.3 million jobs lost". [4] The main beneficiaries to this trend have been Mexico and south East Asia. To put this in perspective, consider this phenomenon, 40% of IBM's total workforce resides in foreign countries and the largest private employer in Singapore is General Electric, which just finished building a $150 million Hungarian light bulb factory. [5]

Politicians in developing countries strapped for foreign currency & often poverty ridden are aware of this trend and are standing in line to coax & entice western companies by promising them the lowest labor costs(1996 comparative average compensation for production workers in manufacturing between Mexico & the United States, $17.70 U.S. $1.54 Mexico) [6] and offering corporations virtual tax havens. The governments in developing countries usually assure the western companies protection from union activity through special immunity provisions, or may simply squash any noisemakers by any means necessary, in any case in many of such countries, protection laws for employees are essentially non-existent. The first dilemma borne out of this trend for unions relates to collective bargaining, considering the ease at which corporate owners can relocate production facilities, union organizers are faced to ask themselves how do they effectively engage in collective bargaining with an employer who has at their disposal the option of just closing shop and relocating to a new locale offering enticing capital returns. In some cases, an employer may just be waiting for any labor dispute as an excuse for relocating operations, in fact it is common practice nowadays for companies to openly state their intentions of moving operations. Unions in industrial states with labor intensive manufacturing economic bases & the largest concentrations of unions have been particularly hit hard as illustrated below (selected economic levels from study on effects globalization on U.S. workers).

Share of Total Private Sector Employment in Goods—Producing (%)

Year	US	Indiana	Michigan	Kokomo	South Bend	Jackson
1969	49.5	58.4	57.0	71.8	50.3	60.6
1979	42.85	50.8	49.7	64.6	42.2	52.4
1989	34.0	41.5	38.1	54.8	32.0	41.9
1994	30.7	34.3	30.6	48.2	25.7	30.5

Source: U.S. Census Bureau, Annual Report of County Business Patterns.

Labor & Corporate Response

As the table above illustrates, states that traditionally relied on industrial manufacturing jobs have shown a trend of declining numbers as has the U.S. in a whole. As unions continue to cry foul play on the part of corporate owners who engage in this practice, the owners counter-act stating this is the only way they can survive in this new order of business. They argue that they are simply allocating their capital and resources where they can maximize their returns while following ethical business protocol. Business owners feel the business environment has become so inter-twined and relocation of the production unit comes with the territory in order to stay competitive. Supporters of the global trend utilize the economics 101 theory of "comparative Advantage", asserting that resources will be allocated where they are best utilized & productive.

Unionists on the other hand view such reasoning as simply rhetorical nonsense, and see the real motive of the business owners as taking advantage of the cheap labor while lining their pockets. They contend, the owners are irresponsible and lack corporate morality for abandoning communities that made them what they are and are simply driven by maximizing profits at any cost. Faced with this dilemma, unions have sought creative ways to fight this force despite the lack of legal recourse in most matters of transcontinental commerce. The AFL—CIO union leadership for instance, recognizing the challenges of the global era implemented some new initiatives & policies. it's new policies centered on international competition, which emphasized cross—border union alliances and protections of all workers across the board all over the globe[8]. Some notable cross—border alliances include, the AFL-CIO, Hotel Employees and Restaurant Employees International Union, International Federation of Chemical, Energy, Mine and General Workers, World's Pulp and Paper (represents workers in 21 countries, six continents), all these unions have a common objective of uniting all employees across borders employed by the same multinational parent companies. The effectiveness of cross—border unions however is somewhat limited, besides serving as a solidarity reaffirmation of workers, companies are still engaging in business as usual. Unions have also employed campaign messages such as "Buy American", union leadership has also employed lobbying campaigns to law maker's calling for protectionism in some core industries. The AFL—CIO under the leadership of Sweeney has followed a pro-active strategy by bringing the issue of low wages to the national debate, Sweeney's campaign was instrumental in getting congress to raise the minimum wage. [9] Clearly, the labor movement is not staying put, but rather, taking some initiatives; if anything, to at least slow down this onslaught. As for it's success, that remains to be seen over time. Unions are further constrained and hampered by the absence of any applicable current law with jurisdiction of cross—border commerce and worker rights.

Changing Workforce Dynamics

In the first part of our analysis, we looked at the issue pertaining to U.S. production facilities being shut down and being transplanted in foreign countries, usually developing countries. The ramifications of this trend are clearly evident, this section of the paper is however dedicated to an equally important facet of globalization manifestations, which is often overlooked. The point of reference is the issue relating to the changing workforce make-up of employees particularly in high density immigrant states such as California, Texas, Florida and Arizona, also commonly referred to as border states. The stem of the problem centers on "new immigrants", essentially referring to recent foreign arrivals with an intent to make a new living. The influx of this group in such large urban metro cities such as Las Angeles, Houston, Miami, Phoenix, etc. has been viewed as a blessing or a curse depending on who you talk to. Since this group of "new immigrants" are often from less developed economies and very often find themselves in desperate situations attempting to maintain a daily existence, they are compelled to take up any available position to get income, in most cases they take jobs that are low paying and typically undesirable to the general public. Such jobs include, taxi drivers, landscapers, janitors, hotel housekeeping, fast-food attendants and the likes.

This unusual relationship eventually takes on a domino effect and soon transcends industries as employers realize that they can lower their cost by hiring such employees and boosting their profit margins in the process. Due to this dynamic, union employees become vulnerable as inevitably they consequently face layoffs and things of that nature. It comes as no surprise that the recent trend indicates a sizeable segment of new production facilities seem to favor the sunbelt geographic regions to set up shop, naturally this may have to do with the "work free" statutes that most of these states follow, but for the purpose of this dissertation, we will limit our analysis to the subject matter pertaining to the dynamic of the changing workforce. The statistics on the following page put into perspective the magnitude of this phenomenal in the S. Florida metropolitan area of Miami-Dade County.

Percentage of Foreign-Born Residents in the Miami Standard Metropolitan Statistical Area (SMSA), Selected Years

- 1940 (9.7 %)
- 1950 (12.1 %)
- 1960 (16.9 %)
- 1970 (41.8 %)
- 1980 (53.7 %)
- 1990 (59.7 %)
- 1998 (53.6 %)

Current Population Survey, March 1999.

Percent Immigrant Labor in Various Industries, Miami-Dade County, 1980, 1980, and 1998

- 1980: Eating & Drinking (29.9), Hotel & Lodging(39.8), Apparel(82.6), Nursing Home (19.5)
- 1990:Eating & Drinking (51.3), Hotel & Lodging(65.7), Apparel(85.7), Nursing Home (54.0)
- 1998: Eating & Drinking (67.3), Hotel & Lodging(67.4), Apparel(85-95*), Nursing Home (75-85*)

Sources: For 1980: U.S. Census Bureau 1981, table 227, pp. 941, 942; for 1990: 1990 Census, analysis of Public Use Micro data Sample (PUMS) data; for 1998: Current Population Survey; March 1999, excerpt for apparel and nursing home industries, which are authors' estimates.

H1-B and L-1 dilemma

Another troubling aspect for unions involves the practice of employers attracting foreign workers through the H1-B and L-1 visa programs. This practice became especially widespread in the 1990s following the economic boom and the dot.com explosion.[11] Under this program, U.S. corporations lobbied congress to raise the cap issued on H1-B visas from 65,000 to 195,000 [12]. This move caused extreme outrage and debate all the way to presidential candidates as well as union leadership who contended that this drive was taking away jobs from skilled American workers. The corporations however in their main argument stated there was a shortage of such skilled workers and thus the necessity for foreign workers. It is indeed ironic that the worlds wealthiest economy would lack highly skilled labor, but such was the reasoning presented. The bulk of such foreign workers would come from India, which raised red flags for union activists who viewed this as simply a plot for corporations to get away with hiring cheap skilled labor. It is important to note that the widespread outcry by unions and anti-immigrant right wing groups did payoff as congress did introduce legislation to reduce H1-B numbers to about 80,000 as of 2002 [13].

As we draw to the end of the review, it is evident to see that the issue of U.S. unions and globalization as relating to job relocation and changing dynamics is a very critical matter. Throughout the analytical review, valid concerns and arguments from both parties were raised. The object of this analysis however was not to pick sides on who is right or wrong but rather to present the issue at hand and dissert both vantage points of the parties involved. On the first issue of job relocation, after careful review of all factual background materials, I draw the conclusion business corporations by nature are driven by maximizing returns and thus relocating production facilities fits into the business plan of utilizing the cheapest available labor thereby ensuring maximum profits. One would also say the same logic & reasoning applies to the latter dilemma. As for the outlook on unions fighting this trend, my research leads me to believe the picture is not a bright one, particularly in the absence of legal recourse for unions when it comes to dealing with such issues. It is an unfortunate situation, but one, which unions have to deal with by applying, continued pressure on congress and anyone willing to listen.

REFERENCE NOTES

1. Witney,Fred & Taylor, Benjamin J., Labor Relations Law, 1996. Pg1
2. Witney,Fred & Taylor, Benjamin J., Labor Relations Law, 1996. Pg1
3. Witney,Fred & Taylor, Benjamin J., Labor Relations Law, 1996. Pg23
4. Craver, Charles B., Can Unions Survive,pg45
5. Craver, Charles B., Can Unions Survive,pg45
6 Table1. U.S. Census Bureau
7. Nissen, Bruce., Unions In A Globalize Environment. P212,213
8. Tillman, Ray M., The Transformation of US Unions, 1999. P17
9. Table 2 & 3
10. http:www.atimes.com, Indian IT professionals targeted in US
11 http:www.atimes.com, Indian IT professionals targeted in US
12. http:www.atimes.com, Indian IT professionals targeted in US

CHAPTER V
Financial Analysis

5.1 OBJECTIVES AND COMPETANCES

1.) Provide the student with financial knowledge and analytical skills to make meaningful business decisions, the section therefore presents an overview of financial decision-making. Some key specific objectives in becoming a sound financial analyst are outlined below.

2.) Know function and structure of financial markets

3.) Demonstrate competence in financial ratio analysis

4.) have an understanding of applying discounting methods for present & future value calculations

5.) Apply valuation models to bonds, preferred stocks and common stocks.

6.) understand the different types of risk and relationship to rate of returns.

7.) understand the concept of weighted average cost of capital

8.) Utilize capital budgeting methods such as net present & internal rate of return

9.) utilize financial forecasting and planning techniques

10.) incorporate working capital management to cash management, credit management, inventory management and short-term financing.

5.2 OVERVIEW OF FINANCIAL MANAGEMENT

The field of financial management is essentially comprised of three areas. The first area relates to *money and capital markets*. In this concentration an analyst will primarily deal with the securities market and financial institutions. The second area lays emphasis on *investments,* the stem of this area deals with making investment decisions both on an individual basis and organizational level. The investment manager through his or her expertise makes the tough decisions on which securities would best suite the respective investment portfolio. The third and final area is *financial management*, which involves business decisions within firms and other business entities. As one can see, all three fields are closely intertwined thus it is very important that successful financial managers have a good understanding of each area.

5.3 CREDIT POLICY

An effective company credit policy usually will have the following staples.

- Solid Credit standards
- Clear credit terms emphasizing the credit period & terms of cash discounts
- A detailed Collection policy
- Five "C's of Credit: Character, Capacity, Capital, Collateral & Conditions

Monitoring Accounts Receivable

- Average Collection Period(ACP) or Days of Sales Outstanding (DSO)
- Aging Schedules, Analyzing Changes in Credit Policy.

CREDIT POLICY VARIABLES: Effects & Changes

VARIABLE and CHANGE	Effect on DSO(Days sales outstanding)	Effect on Sales	Effect on BAD DEBT EXPENSE
Credit Period Shortened	Decreases	May Decrease	Indeterminate effects
Cash Discount Increased	Decreases	May Increase	Indeterminate effects
Credit Standards Tightened	Decreases	May Decrease	Decreases
Collection Policy Tightened	Decreases	May Decrease	Decreases

* DSO (Days sales outstanding)

Inventory and the Economic Ordering Quantity (EOQ)

1   Assume that you are examining the Inventory practices of your firm. You believe that order sizes may be larger than necessary. You decide to look at one key product. For this product, you have been placing orders for 5,000 units. Each unit costs $3.20 and there is a fixed cost of $100 per order. Sales for this product are 25,000 units per year, and are uniform throughout the year. Annual carrying cost is 20% of Inventory value.

a. What is the current cost of inventory?

Carrying (holding) cost:

Step 1. Determine average cost = 5,000/2 = 2,500 units

Step 2. Carrying cost = 2,500 x $3.20 x .20 = $1,600

Step 3. Ordering cost = orders per year = 25,000/5,000 = 5

Ordering cost = 5 x 100 = $500

Step 4. Total cost = 1,600 + 500 = 2,100

b. Now use the EOQ model to determine the optimal ordering quantity; and calculate the new cost of inventory based on this ordering quantity.

EOQ = square root of [(2xFxS)/ (CxP)] where:

F is the fixed cost per order

S is the annual sales per order

C is the annual carrying cost expressed as a% of inventory value

P is the purchase price per unit of inventory

For this example, = square root of [(2x100x25,000)/(.20 x 3.2) = 2,795 order size

Average inventory = 2,795/2 = 1,397.5

Orders per year = 25,000/2,795 = 8.94454 times per year

Costs: carrying cost = 1,397.5 x 3.20 x .20 = $894

Ordering cost = 8.94 x 100 = $894

Total cost: $1,788

Notes:

.   Mathematically, if we use the exact average inventory and the exact orders per year, then the carrying cost and the ordering cost will be equal.

.   If we make small adjustments to the number of orders per year and the size of the orders, then the carrying cost & ordering cost will be close, but not equal.

. Note this model can be modified to include safety stocks.

5.4 CASH CONVERSION CYCLE ILLUSTRATION

40 DAYS (Between A & B)

35 DAYS (From B to C)

A). BUY

B).SELL

MATERIALS

LABOR

C). COLLECT

Inventory Conversion period: 40days(A to B)

Receivables Collection Period(DSO/ACP): 35 days (B to C)

Cash conversion cycle: 40 + 35—15 = <u>60days</u>.

5.5 PRACTICAL DEFINATIONS

Working Capital refers to current assets used in operations.

Net working capital: (current assets—current liabilities.)

Net operating working capital: (Cash + A/R + Inventory)—(A/P + Accruals)

Working Capital and the Cash Conversion Cycle

Firm X has annual sales of $720,000 and cost of goods sold is $288,000

Therefore: Sales per Day = 720,000/360 = $2000

Cost of goods sold per day = 288,000/360 = $800

Given this information from the balance sheet:

Account Receivables: $70,000

Inventory: $50,000

Payables: $12,000

Inventory Conversion Period:

Inventory/(daily sales) = 50,000/2,000 = 25 days [implies 25 days worth of inventory]

Receivables Collection Period (or DSO) :

Receivables/(daily sales) = 70,000/2000 = 35 days

Payables Deferral Period:

IPayables/(cost of goods sold per day) = 12,000/800 = 15 days

Cash Conversion Cycle:

[implies from the time you pay for something and get back return$$$]

(25 days + 35 days—15 days) = 45 days

Determining the amount of working capital the firm must finance:

Multiply the Length of Cash Conversion Cycle by the Cost of Goods sold

That is:

Length of CashConversion Cycle X Cost of Goods Sold per Day

(45 days x 800 = $36,000)

5.6 COST OF TRADE CREDIT

Credit Terms: 3/10, net 60

Implies if cash discount is accepted, then purchase price is reduced by 3%, and payment must be made in 10 days.

If cash discount is not taken, then the whole amount must be paid in 60 days.

Given this circumstance, if a $100.00 purchase is made with the 3% cash discount (derived from the 3/10 terms), total amount paid within 10 days is $97.00 However, if cash discount is not taken, then the $100.00 would be due in 60 days. This translates into $3 in interest for a 50-day period(60—10 days).

$3 in interest on a $97 purchase, which is 3/97 = 3.09%

However this only covers a 50-day (60—10) period, to get an annual figure:

[assuming a 360 day year] 360/50 = 7.2

Therefore, 3.09% x 7.2 = 22.3% annual interest

% Cost of trade credit formula (general terms) =

Discount%/(1—Discount%) x 360/ (total credit period—discount period) .

5.7 IMPORTANT FINANCIAL RATIOS

LIQUIDITY RATIOS

1. Current Ratio: Current Assets /Current Liabilities (*measures ability to meet short term debts/obligations)*

2. Quick Ratio or (Acid Test): Current Assets—Inventory/ Current Liabilities (*measure of meeting short term debts w/out relying on sell of inventory)*

ASSET MANAGEMENT RATIOS

1. Inventory Turnover Ratio: Sales / Inventories (*how well is firm managing inventories)*

2. Days Sales Outstanding(DSO), also called "average collection period" (ACP), used to appraise accounts receivable.

DSO: Receivables/ Average sales per day = Receivables/Annual sales/360

3. Fixed Asset Turnover ratio: Sales/ Net Fixed Assets (*how well is company uses its plant & equipment*

4. Total Asset Turnover Ratio: Sales/Total Assets (*measures turnover of al assets or capital intensity*)

5. Operating Capital Requirement Ratio: Operating Capital/ Sales (*relationship between Sales & operat. Cap.*)

DEBT MANAGEMENT(LEVERAGE) RATIOS

1. Debt Ratio: Total Debt/ Total Assets (*percentage of funds from creditors*

   how heavily financed is firm)

2. Debt to Equity Ratio: Total Debt/Total Equity (*compares borrowed funds to stockholder funds*)

3. Times Interest Earned (TIE) ratio: EBIT/Interest Charges

   * *where EBIT is earnings before interest & taxes, this ratio*

   Measures the level to which operating income can decline

   Before firm is unable to meet it's annual interest cost.

4. Fixed Charge Coverage Ratio: *similar to above ratio but goes on to include lease payments as well as sinking fund payments.*

   (EBIT + Lease Payments/ Interest charges + Lease payments) + (Sinking Fund Payments)/(1-Tax Rate)

PROFITABILITY RATIOS

1. Profit Margin on Sales: Net Income avail. To Common Stockholders/Sales

2. Basic earning ratio (BEP): EBIT / Total Assets (*shows raw earning power before taxes and leverage*)

3. Operating profit margin after taxes: NOPAT(net opt. Profit after taxes)/Sales (*shows how profitable operations are after taxes*).

4. Return on Total Assets: Net Income avail. To Common Stockholders/Total Assets (*measures return on total assets after interest and taxes*)

5. Return on common Equity: Net Income avail. To Common Stockholders

   * *measures rate of return on stockholders investment*

MARKET VALUE RATIOS

1. Price/Earnings (P/E) ratio: Price per share/Earnings per share (*how much investors are willing per $ of reported earnings I.e. how market values stock*)

2. Earnings per Share: Net Profit After tax—Preferred stock Dividends/Average number of shares outstanding. (*how much profit each share of common stock earns*).

3. Book Value per share: Common equity / Shares Outstanding (*how investors regard company*)

. Market/Book ratio: Market price per share/Book Value per share

When dealing with ratios, it is important to place numbers being utilized in comparable terms so as to get accurate measures. To do this , the consumer price index or CPI as it is commonly referred to is normally utilized. This typically gives a base year as a point of reference for inflation. This is illustrated below:

Current dollars x = CPI base year/CPI current yearBase year dollars

CHAPTER VI
Ethics in Business

6.1 Overall Objectives

This section offers the student with an examination of common ethical issues and conflicts managers often encounter within their organizations and how to best deal with such issues utilizing logical ethical thinking. As such codes of ethics, international ethics, moral issues, environmental ethics and various other concepts are analyzed. The global era today is a constant changing and often complicated dynamic, thus this section attempts to offer the student a broad overview to help them become better managers and leaders. The section opens with an overview of the United States Constitution given this is a section dealing with ethics, it is imperative that students always have an understanding of their constitutional rights. The section closes with a paper the author researched on the IMF practices with Africa as relates to ethical principles.

Why have a Code of Ethics?
- to define accepted/acceptable behaviors;
- to promote high standards of practice;
- to provide a benchmark for members to use for self evaluation;
- to establish a framework for professional behavior and responsibilities;
- as a vehicle for occupational identity;
- as a mark of occupational maturity;"

Source: website of http://www.calsca.com/ethics_lscabc.htm)

IMC USA Code of Ethics

All IMC USA members pledge in writing to abide by the Institute's Code of Ethics. Their adherence to the Code signifies voluntary assumption of self-discipline above and beyond the requirements of law. Key provisions of the Code specify:

Clients

- Members will serve their clients with integrity, competence, and objectivity, using a professional approach at all times, and placing the best interests of the client above all others.
- Members will establish realistic expectations of the benefits and results of their services.
- Members will treat all client information that is not public knowledge as confidential, will prevent it from access by unauthorized people, and will not take advantage of proprietary or privileged information, either for use by them, their firm or another client, without the client's permission.
- Members will avoid conflicts of interest, or the appearance of such, and will disclose to a client any circumstances or interests that might influence their judgment and objectivity.
- Members will refrain from inviting an employee of an active or inactive client to consider alternative employment without prior discussion with the client.

Engagements

- Members will only accept assignments which they possess the expertise to perform, and will only assign staff with the requisite expertise.
- Members will ensure that before accepting any engagement, a mutual understanding of the objectives, scope, work plan, and fee arrangements has been established.
- Members will offer to withdraw from a consulting engagement when their objectivity or integrity may be impaired.

Fees

- Members will agree in advance with a client on the basis for fees and expenses, and will charge fees and expenses that are reasonable, legitimate and commensurate with the services delivered and the responsibility accepted.

- Members will disclose to their clients in advance any fees or commissions that they receive for equipment, supplies or services they could recommend to their clients.

Profession

- Members will respect the individual and corporate rights of clients and consulting colleagues, and will not use proprietary information or methodologies without permission.

- Members will represent the profession with integrity and professionalism in their relations with their clients, colleagues and the general public.

- Members will report violations of this Code to the Institute, and will ensure that other consultants working on behalf of the member abide by this Code.

The Institute of Management Consultants USA, Inc. (IMC USA) adopted its first Code of Ethics in 1968. Since that time IMC USA has modified the wording of the Code for additional clarity and relevance to clients. The current Code was approved February 22, 2002. It is consistent with the International Code of Professional Conduct published by the International Council of Management Consulting Institutes (ICMCI) of which IMC USA is a founding member.

Members who apply for the CMC (Certified Management Consultant) designation must pass a written examination on the application of the IMC USA Code of Ethics to client service. The CMC mark is awarded to consultants who have met high standards of education, experience, competence and professionalism.

ETHICAL ISSUES & BUSINESS:

6.2 Environmental Philosophy

Latest thinking in environmental philosophy seems to have taken a non-exploitive ethic. The latest thinking follows the premise that human beings must not take on the environment as dominators, but rather as generic participants in the whole dynamic. Following such thoughts, new ideas which somewhat take an eccentric view have evolved the notion of *deep ecology* which essentially proclaims the immediate halt of domination of human beings on the environment. Some of the more radical concepts have gone as far as promoting drastic measures including indulging in lawlessness in order to save the environment.

Such views challenge the older views, which basically considered the environment as a means to wealth, which was to be exploited without consequence in order to attain as much wealth as possible. As such, these new views are drastically at odds with the older views which centered on utilitarian doctrines that professed, that despite the effects of pollution being harmful, the social costs passed on to society were more beneficial therefore validating pollution.

6.3 Risk Analysis

Risk analysis pertaining to human risks typically is a function of two processes. The first process involves the collective factors of risk assessment, which heavily relies upon scientific and technical inputs. Harmful effects are identified through collection of quantitative and objective data. Having identified the associated dangers, a series of tests on laboratory animals are conducted in order to quantify the risks. The second part of risk analysis is characterized as risk management. Essentially this is a non-scientific process based on the law, politics, economics and ethics. Proponents of risk analysis regard its heavy use of scientific and technical tools as a major strength. By the same token, some disadvantages of this method are the physiological differences presented by lab animals to humans, as such critics argue that relying on animal tests may lead to unreliable conclusions

Cost benefit analysis is the tail end of the risk analysis process where associated costs and benefits of a proposed action are compared. Typically, such analysis involves assigning monetary coefficients in order to facilitate comparisons. If it is determined that the benefits exceed the costs, then the proposed action is deemed favorably and vice-versa.

Advantages of cost benefit analysis

- Methodical
- Optimal alternatives in terms of economic inputs
- Acts as rational measure to emotional arguments
- Helpful to regulators in determining the most efficient policy

Disadvantages:

- Determining cost/benefit values difficult & controversial
- Valuation of human life complex/controversial
- May result in trade-offs of environmental quality
- Subjects of regulation may pass costs to innocent parties by raising prices of their end products in order to cover their costs.

6.4 Global Competition

U.S. Global competition strengths:

- world leader in super-computers
- software engineering
- artificial intelligence
- computer-aided design
- engineering, telecommunications, genetic engineering & rocket propulsion

Weaknesses:

- consumer products
- semiconductors

steel, automobiles & machine tools

One strategy that proved successful and effective was reduction in costs. This included lateral moves where partnerships with suppliers were embraced in creating long-term relationships, which subsequently created greater efficiency, lower costs, greater profit margins and a competitive edge. Similarly, integration of departments within the organization resulted in lower costs and allowed emphasis on product quality control and development. Outsourcing is another strategy that was effective. In this instance, the organization is able to utilize cheap labor in certain locales particularly third-world countries thereby drastically reducing their costs and thus enhancing their competitiveness. Other cost cutting strategies include direct foreign investments.

The second area of success pertains to improvements in productivity through mergers and alliances with the assumption that such actions foster efficiency by sharing risks.

Host country Fears:

a). Human rights abuses—governments fear that multinational companies have a tendency of disregarding such rights. Common abuses cited include those pertaining to, child labor abuses, and exploitation of local workers by paying low wages.

b). Environmental concerns—multinationals assume less social responsibility and in turn pollute the host nations environment without regard to the consequences.

c). Protectionism issues—host governments fear multinationals present unfair competition to local industries and eventually may drive them out of business.

d). Cultural & Ethical differences.

To counter these and other fears, governments impose measures such as restrictions in the form of trade barriers, outright trade bans, and institute quotas on imports. Despite these underlying conflicts, some notable benefits result from such partnerships as summarized below:

- provide local employment
- transfer of technology
- boosts standard of living
- enhances foreign exchange reserves
- opens foreign markets

6.5 PAC's, NAFTA, Worker & Consumer Rights, Title VII

Business interests attempt to influence the political environment by utilizing political action committees, commonly called PAC's. They take advantage of a legislative loophole that allows for organizations to set-up PACs. In this manner , they are able to solicit contributions. Business interests also employ brokering and bundling techniques to facilitate contributions to candidates. Another common avenue used involves donations by means of soft money. Finally, donations into the political arena are made through unlimited independent expenditures such as campaign advertisements.

Current campaign laws call for full public disclosure of contributions and expenditures. In addition, restricted contributions by individuals and PACs to candidates are allowed. These limits are guided by an assortment of spelled-out legal limits.

By making contributions, business organizations hope to gain access, influence and receive favors to promote their corporate interests. I believe these are dangerous trends in view of current practices, which need to be reformed. It seems current legislation is ineffective as business interests always find loopholes to side step the law. The greatest danger I see is a situation where the fine line is crossed and politicians become pawns of business.

NAFTA .

1). NAFTA is a treaty embarked by the United States, Canada, and Mexico which created the largest trading bloc in the world with over 400 million customers. The primary objective of this agreement was to promote trade by lifting certain barriers such as tariffs, duties and so forth. The treaty was to benefit all parties involved by expanding GDP and creating jobs.

2). NAFTA Skeptics

- US will loose jobs to Mexico due to cheap labor.
- Will result in lower wages for low-wage jobs in the U.S.
- Prone to worker rights violations
- Environmental degradation in places like Mexico lacking strict standards.

3). NAFTA Proponents argue that free trade is necessary for economic growth.

- Goods exported to member countries will in turn support jobs in home country.
- Increases GDP

4). The numbers suggest NAFTA is proportionately a minor factor in the American economy and likely more significant for the Mexican economy.

5).The political & social arguments seem more exaggerated than the implicit economic impact.

6).Time needs to be allowed to see what direction the current NAFTA arrangement takes before considering expansion.

Consumer Rights

The consumer movement has been very instrumental in making business more conscious and cognitive to consumer views in general. Due to various concerns by consumers and advocates, the business community to some degree acknowledges these groups as major stakeholders. As such, many corporations in their corporate statements specifically make it a point to address customer satisfaction as a primary goal. Some of the major landmarks of this movement can be traced to the early 1960s by pioneers such as Rachel Carson. Other early notable figures in this movement include, Ralph Nader, John F. Kennedy, and Peter Drucker. In the 1980s, Peters and Waterman in their book, "In Search of Excellence" reinforced commitment to this movement. Ralph Nader's influence over the years has pressured congress to respond by stepping up efforts of regulatory agencies protecting consumer rights. Ralph Nader's influence though has diminished as corporations and the republican congress found ways of slowing this movement. Many other significant advocate groups exist and are always keeping a keen eye.

Important authorities and legislation today are in place to protect consumers. These include groups such as "The Consumer Product Safety

Commission", which was created in 1972 to protect consumers in terms of safety and so on. This agency regulates a wide assortment of consumer products. The National Highway Traffic Safety Administration, created in 1966 is concerned with automobile & truck safety. Several other such agencies exist acting as shields to consumer rights.

Worker Rights

Workers today are still demanding the traditional concerns such as safety at work, medical benefits, equal treatment, better wages and so forth. The movement today is not as passionate as was the case in earlier years. The nature of today's workers demands has drastically changed, where as in the past workers were typically concerned about stability and loyalty from employers in terms of job security, recent trends fostering global economies wiped out that philosophy. Today, employers are accustomed to downsizing and turbulent forces at the work place. As such, today's employees have become savvy and less concerned about job security and company loyalty, instead they focus on improving their marketability through on-going training. Workers like employers have also developed less loyal to organizations, and are quick to move to another job offering more rewards. Recognizing this dynamic, companies routinely encourage self-improvement and will offer sponsorship toward training as they constantly seek a highly skilled streamlined workforce. These new rights have been fostered due to competitive and global forces where companies have to keep reorganizing their structures to stay afloat.

Title VII

Title VII has been interpreted as requiring preferential treatment through its underlying theme, which prohibits discrimination in any aspect of employment. The Supreme Court has struggled with the issue surrounding the interpretation of Title VII mainly from a philosophical and constitutional right standpoint. The philosophical argument implies Title VII goes against the ideal of equal opportunity in essence. Another source of conflict is those who contend that Title VII undermines the principle of achievement based on merit and as such constitutes a violation of individual rights. The Supreme Court finds itself entangled with arguments of people who feel their rewards have been taken away from them despite not practicing any discrimination behavior.

On the other hand, the Supreme Court is confronted with an alternate set of arguments centering on utilitarian considerations, which advocate that title VII benefits everyone by fully utilizing all available talent and thus creating political stability. Other arguments include those relating to the ethical theories of justice and ethical theories of rights. In the end, no easy answer exists with this issue, on balance I think Title VII is required and essential for utilitarian reasons as well as for ensuring everyone has equal access and opportunity.

6.6 Corporate governance

Critics of corporate governance feel that the performance of board members in boosting equity investment is inadequate and in many instances these board members do not take into consideration the views of employees, stakeholders, society, etc in their decisions. In fact critics feel most such decisions are made contrary to the stakeholders concerns. Critics also point out that board members are grossly over paid relative to the functions they perform, many feel the board members do not spend enough time on company matters but merely act as rubber stamps of the company's executive staff.

Some of the suggested reforms include calls to evaluate the performance of the board of directors. This suggestion stipulates that while some boards engage in some sought of evaluation, usually such evaluations are not objective and refrain from negative feedback but rather are simply self-serving. Another suggested reform calls for the separation of the CEO and the Board Chairman. Advocates of this suggestion believe this would be an effective way of diluting the power base. However, I feel even if these suggested measures were to be adopted, their impact would be minimal as these boards exert a lot of power and influence to circumvent the effects.

6.7 International Monetary Fund & Africa: Ethics Examined

The African continent is one graced with abundant natural wealth but is always seemingly at crossroads with its quest to rise from the grips of poverty and human catastrophes. The last decade has been particularly brutal and with devastation of epic proportions. The continent is at a critical desperate point. To understand and shed some light into how and why the continent is in this position and continues to struggle, this review examines the relationship between Africa and the International Monetary Fund. The review further addresses the issue in terms of the underlying ethical practices employed by the IMF in its lending and general practices. The review takes a look at the nature and consequence of this relationship keeping the ethical concerns at the forefront. In part, the analysis focuses on four ethical questions relating to:

- Structural Adjustments
- IMF as a driving force for debt
- Exploitation
- IMF interests and motivations.

The relationship between Africa and the IMF has never been at the center stage of controversy more so than now. At the forefront of this ensuing outrage are the practices the IMF is being accused of employing toward these poverty stricken nations. The main issue echoed by activist groups and the African leadership being that pertaining to conditions IMF imposes to these nations in order for them to attain loans. Many have argued that so often these conditions are not only unfair but, also amount to ineffective policy. Further more, African nations insist these imposed structural adjustments are harmful and counteractive. These nations further contend that these same imposed policies are driving them into more debt and at a local level responsible for social unrest, unemployment and economic degradation.

IMF sees the situation differently and stands by its policies and practices. As opposed to the critics views, IMF sees the problem as a function of host countries engaged in mismanagement and bad policy selection. As one may expect, this is clearly a complex subject matter with so many variables. However, this paper will primarily look at the ethical issues as relates to policy. As we explore this sometimes fascinating, sometimes troubling dilemma, the author employs all available resources and heavily relies on factual secondary sources in addition to his firsthand personal experiences.

Literature Review

This subject matter has received extensive attention from researchers of all backgrounds. Most of the material uncovered was from the 1990s onward with the vast majority conducted by non-governmental organizations. The IMF itself was a great resource especially with statistical information. Equally resourceful was material from activist groups and vigilante watch groups. It seems most of the material outside of the IMF and World Bank took an anti-IMF position. For the most part, most resources presented an objective point of view.

Tale of the IMF & African courtship

The ethical question that arises is a derivative of increasing inequalities primarily between the developed and least developed nations. According to the United Nations Development Program [1], global inequality is worse now than ever before. In 1950 the gap between the richest and the poorest country was about 35 to one, while by 1992 it had widened to 72 to one. As such per capita incomes in these poor countries has continued to decline in the last decade, particularly in sub-Saharan Africa. This is a very disturbing trend and sadly, the disparity continues to widen.

As a youngster growing up in Zambia in the 70s and 80s, I remember a very different Africa than what we have seen in the last decade. Indeed poverty and other associated social ills were apparent then, but the comparison to today is inconceivable and simply pales to the present sub-Saharan Africa. I can recall then president, Dr Kenneth Kaunda vehemently opposed to the IMF programs. What was in place then was more of a socialist approach where government was essentially central in providing all social services such as education, health-care, and so forth. Generally people were significantly better off in many aspects. Government agencies may not have been run as efficiently as those in the developed nations, but nonetheless were able to provide basic needs such as medical treatment, elementary & higher education, social security and various other such services at no cost. People for all intensive purposes had a sense of empowerment and hope.

However, under growing pressures to secure vital foreign exchange, which is a lifeline for many of these African countries, desperation and necessity would call for drastic measures. A vast majority of these countries had been able to cope well and manage to sustain a reasonable marginal self-sustaining existence, however a host of factors including the continued decline in commodity prices (which accounted for almost all foreign exchange revenues) left the African leadership scratching their heads. Whether coincidentally or a case of doomed destiny, the IMF was suddenly in the picture, thus a beginning of an intricate courtship. This courtship would eventually transcend all odds and end up in matrimony. This was no marriage that called for a honeymoon, time was of the essence, and so it was, a union was matriculated. From the get go, this relationship was rocky and as intense as a championship chase match. One might in fact describe it similar to a dysfunctional marriage scripted out of Hollywood and conceived in a Las Vegas drive-through establishment by two intoxicated partners.

Under its articles for lending funds,[2] the IMF was quick and swift to spell out an assortment of conditions that had to be met in order to process and facilitate the release of funds. This is one area where some ethical questions on the part of the IMF come into play, which will be further examined in the latter part of the paper. However questionable the motives and intentions of the IMF, indeed they could have very well been well meant, however what is evident are the harmful implications such tactics have had. Over the years most of the African leadership relented to the spelled out terms, therefore going about implementing a series of economic and monetary changes such as, deregulation, opening up markets to foreign firms, constant devaluation of currencies, etc. All said, these adjustments would have devastating consequences of catastrophic proportions, basically causing many of the economies to self-implode.

The IMF on the hand in its defense of its policies contends the catastrophic turn of events are not a result of their policies but rather a function of bad governance at the local level and gross mismanagement at the local administrative level. The argument is a two-fold argument with each side engaged in finger pointing much like a squabbling couple. Revisiting the subject of initial intentions of the IMF in my estimation presents us with an unquestionable ethical dilemma. One indeed might ask, *did the IMF engage in unethical behavior by imposing these structural adjustments?* This is a question among others we shall address and continue to revisit in this paper in trying to ascertain reasonable answers. As with many ethical questions, one might contend that the answer is only as good as the bearer, in other words, reflects the bearers inclinations. Thus said, let me assure the readers that as the author, my assertions and opinions are simply a derivative of facts examined and from personal experiences. (income disparities and poverty concentrations).[3]

Imposed Structural Adjustments

The subject relating to IMF sanctioned structural adjustments has caused the greatest uproar by far. Non-so evident is the escalating disdain for these adjustments than the recent influx of protests mounted by activist groups at scheduled IMF global meeting locations. The outrage in many instances has strayed from peaceful protests to violent clashes, in fact some extremist groups have gone as far as staging intricate planned sabotage activities. Recent clashes at the WTO, IMF and World Bank summit[4] seemed to have set a wave of defiance directed toward these groups. Following are some examples of scores of protests that have ensued: The IMF & World Bank summit in Prague drew large crowds in arms[5,]. At a Washington, D.C. summit, protesters exceeded 30,000.[6]. In Lusaka, Zambia where officials from the IMF and Zambian parliament members were meeting to address poverty reduction, the scenes and drama that followed are narrated in the excepts below from the Times of Zambia.[7]

LUSAKA, April 26 (Oneworld.Net)—Scores of anti-International Monetary Fund (IMF) protestors were dispersed by armed riot police in Zambia's capital Lusaka yesterday after they attempted to picket outside a hotel where IMF and Zambian officials were meeting. Protestors, brought together by leading women's rights groups opposed to IMF and World Bank policies which attempt to price open markets— accused the Fund of bringing misery to poor countries by imposing strict conditions on their economies, which benefit only the rich.

"IMF policies are killing us, especially women and children," said Emily Sikazwe of Women for Change shortly after the aborted demonstration.

Officials from the IMF and the Zambian parliament were meeting to discuss their partnership for growth and poverty reduction. Speaker of the National Assembly, Amussa Mwanamwambwa, told IMF representatives that Zambia's continued indebtedness to the IMF had resulted in a perception that multilateral creditors were obstacles to the attainment of domestic socio-economic needs.

"It is important for the IMF to use this {visit as an} opportunity to explain before the people's elected representatives the IMF s difficulties and objections to the worldwide call for total debt cancellation," Mwamamwambwa said.

The IMF says its lending schemes were broadened recently through the establishment of the Poverty Reduction and Growth Facility. The scheme to cut poverty would be planned by government with input from civil society, said IMF Assistant Director for Africa Reinold Van Til.

Why all this outrage one might wonder? To get a firm understanding of the underlying issue, it is important to go back and examine the pertaining institutional functions of the IMF.[8,pg. 3&4 IMF supplement] In its provisions, the IMF gives itself a broad jurisdiction over nations requiring loans. For instance, the IMF can demand and monitor exchange arrangements. This broad mandate over policy is what Sub-Saharan nations resent in that they feel they are not able to institute their own policies better suited to their agendas, but instead continuously being forced into harmful structural adjustments. Their debt on the other hand keeps growing by leaps and bounds, what they call the debt trap. Due to their need for foreign exchange, they find themselves in an uncompromising situation where they keep borrowing at inflated interest rates while their cumulative debt balloons. This leads to the 2nd ethical question I present. "Recognizing the vulnerable position of these nations, how can the IMF justify keep driving them deeper into debt while subjecting them to outrageous interest rates, even in cases where the principle owed has been paid over and over in interest charges". A recent World Bank Report on Global debt revealed the following disturbing points.[8]

1. The IMF extracted a net $1 billion from Africa in 1997 and 1998, reversing the trend of the last five years. At the same time, it spent billions bailing out bankers in East Asian crisis economies.

2. Developing countries paid back $13 for every $1 they received in grants in 1998, up from $9 in 1996.

3. Commodity prices have plunged, crippling the poorest countries ability to repay foreign debt.

4. Despite borrowing less than they paid back in 1998, total debt in developing countries rose again by $150 billion to a new total of almost $2.5 trillion.

Structural adjustments cause an even greater ill in terms of social and human costs. The human tales at face value present a very disturbing picture, indeed I have experienced first hand on a personal level the human impact and ultimate cost. Some of the most commonly employed structural adjustments include:

a): Privatization

This occurs when governments are required to sell government owned entities to the private market, sometimes referred to as privatization. Such measures usually lead to mass unemployment in the long run, substantial pay reductions by private companies,

degradation of services previously offered at subsidized or for the most part at no cost by the government, particularly social services such as health and education. These policies also thwart local enterprises that are not able to compete with foreign companies.

b): User Fees

These policies call for charging for services such as medical care, education and social security. While they may be better suited for developed nations, such programs are ineffective and very harmful in poor countries as illustrated by some testimonials presented in the paper later. This particular policy unlike others has caused the greatest human impact.

c): Promotion of exports

While it may seem like a good policy on paper, when put in practice this practice can be destructive particularly to domestic traditional subsistence farmers who are forced to farm more export oriented crops. In many cases, they end up being driven off their lands to make room for large commercial farmers. In addition to displacing rural farmers, it promotes hunger and destitution because consumer crops which fed local populations are replaced by commercial crops that yield high margins such as tobacco.

d): Devaluation of Currency

Countries are constantly requested to devalue their currencies as a condition for receiving loans. Naturally, this drives cost of imports high by lowering the purchasing power, which eventually leads to lower standards of living, social unrest, inflation, unemployment and a host of other ills. These are just a few of the controversial restructuring policies. The following exhibit presents some testimonials echoed by common folks.[9]

Globalization

This follows our third ethical dilemma, which contends *that western countries gain at the expense of developing countries.* The share of income of global transactions is less than 2% accounting for African markets and continues to decline.[10] The polarization of views on globalization couldn't be better illustrated by the opinions of the Indian Finance minister and the World Bank chief executive both commenting on the same subject.[11] Jashwan Sinha, Indian finance minister had this to say, globalization must be managed in the best interests of everyone in the world, especially the poorer countries. James Wolfensohn, the head of the World Bank echoed these sentiment, globalization was probably inevitable and protestors were wrong to think that it was a process, which was under the control of international institutions. Such contrasting views simply further illustrate the complexity of such matters. Basically, two schools of thought almost always at odds with each other comprise the main players.

Third World leadership usually asserts that the IMF and its likes are institutions controlled by a few wealthy countries with destructive intentions designed to further enrich these already wealthy countries while destroying third world nations. The IMF however sees the situation in a different light and offers the explanation that they are simply lending money at cost with the interest of African nations at the centerpiece. The ethical dilemma here in part is :*whose interest is the IMF concerned with and at what cost?* I raise this question in part because it is at the cornerstone of the globalization issue. As pointed out earlier, the IMF through its statements and press releases contends that globalization is an inevitable function of the market forces, therefore distancing itself from the conflict. However, one would wonder whether past actions support this notion. Similarly, the IMF discredits accusations by African leadership that the IMF is essentially a loan-shark entity exploiting and crippling them. Its assertion remains firm stating that it views itself as an organization strongly committed to assisting these poor countries in their plight to end their social ills and rise from poverty.

As we draw to the end of our quest in our exploration of the troubled marriage between the IMF and Africa, indeed one can agree that this union is a complex one with so many variables. It is ironic that as I was conducting research on this subject, all my emotions were evoked, whether through laughter, saddens, contempt, intrigue, etc. such was the tale of this compilation. However, one thing that cannot be overlooked is that there are some troubling transgressions involved, particularly the human costs. Throughout the paper we raised some ethical questions and now we try to conceptualize some answers. The object of the paper was not point fingers or pick sides, but rather point out some questionable ethical practices. On the first issue which centers on structural adjustments, I think it is clear some of the practices employed particularly the four we focused on in chapter 2, under the key adjustments constitute unethical practices on the part of the IMF. Similarly, on the second question raised regarding debt, I thought for the most part the IMF acted irresponsibly with unethical persuasions. On the third question dealing with exploitation by western countries, I failed to see any ethical malpractice. Likewise on the question of whose interest the IMF was acting on and at what cost, I found it difficult to raise any ethical concerns even if one was to assume IMF was acting on behalf of other interests, if anything what can be said is that this is a case of profit with hints of greed but isolated from ethical concerns. I should note the IMF should be commended on some recent steps taken in instituting debt relief to various African countries, that in itself is a big step.[12]

Recommendation & Implications

The IMF clearly has work to do given all the issues raised, most critical in need would be the revision and overhaul of loan conditions, however one group that cannot be left out of this equation are some of the corrupt African Leadership who perpetuate some of these sad manifestations to continue. This analytical review did not indulge on the subject of the rampant corruption on the continent, but clearly that has a large role into the problems, thus deserving a special mention. The implications are grave naturally with sad human impacts that will affect many generations to come.

REFERENCE NOTES

[1]. United Nations Global Program. (2001).
Retrieved from group data base
www.un.org
[2] International Monetary Fund Report. (2001)
Retrieved from group data base
www.imf.org
[3]. World Bank(2001)
Retrieved from group data base
www.worldbank.org
[4]. World Development Movement Report. (2001). States of Unrest.
Retrieved from group data base
www.pages.hotbot.com
[5]. Denouncing Global Capitalism. (2001)
Retrieved from group data base
www.news.bbc.co.uk
[6]. Denouncing Global Capitalism. (2001)
Retrieved from group data base
news.bbc.co.uk
[7]. Times of Zambia. (April, 26, 2000)
Retrieved from:
www.oneworld.com
[8]. International Monetary Fund Report (2001).
Retrieved from group data base
www.imf.org
[9]. Jubilee 2000 Coalition (2001). IMF takes $1 billion from Africa
Retrieved from group data base www.jubilie2000uk.org
[10 & 11]. BBC News online(2000) World Bank Development Committee.
Retrieved from group database
www.news,bbc.co.uk
[12].BBC News online(2000) World Bank Development Committee.
Retrieved from group database
www.news,bbc.co.uk

CHAPTER VII
Organizational Behavior

7.1 overview

Management thought is an ever-evolving field of study as organizations at all levels seek to find the right balance between theory and functionality in enhancing maximum returns. Indeed it can be quite said that management thought as a concept is a true mosaic. Four distinct areas encompass management thought transition. The first era is what is referred to as the **classical or scientific** era. This era can be credited for such prolific theorists such as Henri Fayol, Frederick Taylor and Max Weber. The contribution of these three men is daunting, today Frederick Taylor is commonly referred to as the "father of scientific management". Max Weber is called the "father of organizational theory". Last but not least by any means is Henry Favol who many through his prolific studies on increasing productivity is credited as the father of modern day chain factories and large complex organizations. Fayol is well known for his definition of management as a derivative of five functions:

1.) Planning.
2.) Organizing
3.) Commanding
4.) Coordinating
5.) Controlling.

The second era of management thought was the **behavioral era,** this period saw emphasis being placed on the human aspect being incorporated into management which to a larger extent explains the household names to come out of this era. The three main players were Abraham Maslow, Fredrick Herzberg and Clayton Alderfer. Abraham Maslow is today widely known for his "Hierarchy of needs theory". Frederick Herberg is known for his "Two—Factor Theory also referred to as the motivation hygiene theory. Clayton Alderfer tweaked Maslow's Hierarchy theory and came up with the ERG theory. The third era known as the **contemporary era** has the likes of Douglas Mcgregor, Victor Vroom and so forth. Mcgregor of course, is widely known for his Leadership theory which was coined as "Theory X and Theory Y" and was somewhat controversial particularly the notion concerning the theory that implied that employees inherently did not like work and thus must be forced or coerced. Vroom's "expectancy theory" on the other hand stated that employees were motivated to work as a function or probability of reward. The fourth and final era is the **modern era**. In this period we find theorists combining todays challenging global business decisions with past theories. Peter Drucker and Edward Deming are notable theorists of this period, as will be illustrated in the latter part of this section where I present an exploratory analysis into Mr. Edward Deming emphasizing his famous Total Quality Management theory he exported to Japan in the 1950's.

7.2 Overall objectives and competences

As with most discussion material in this text, the primary objective is to acquaint the student with conceptual material relating to the subject matter while presenting the materials in a methodical manner consistent with establishing clarity. It is expected that the student will have some key specific objectives as well. The key areas of organizational behavior include but are not limited to:

1.) Understanding the fundamentals of Organizational Behavior.

2.) Group dynamics

3.) Organizational structure.

4,) Managing & Communication

5.) Cross cultural dimensions

6.) Leadership Qualities

7.) Time Management

8.) Dealing with and overcoming stressful situations

9.) Conceptualizing management theories to practical situations.

These are some of the few specific objectives.

7.3 Overview of selected theorists:

Clayton Alderfer: Research Interests

Human needs: Focused on Existence, Relatedness and Growth.

Organizational Diagnosis: Various articles such as *The invisible director on corporate boards* published in the Harvard Business Review, Nov-Dec 1986 and *Directorship*, which raised questions about how well corporate directors assess the performance of chief executives. Gives reasons for concern and addresses evaluation avoidance. Jun 96, Business Source Elite.

Race Relations: article titled, field experiment for studying race relations embedded in organizations. research study on the psychological effect of data gathering methods in studies on race relations showed that better relationships were established between researchers and respondents if they had the same race, sex and social background. Also found that responsiveness of respondents failed to alter the results of race relations studies. Jan 96, Journal of Organizational Behavior.. *{*member of race and gender balanced consulting teams; very active in trying to change race relations in organizations.*}

Group & Inter group Dynamics: article titled, Understanding embedded inter group relations: a comment on Yammarino and Jung. Points at lack of research to supporting link between leadership and level of analysis, also examines findings about individualism vs. collectivism. march. 98, Journal of Applied Behavioral Science.

Personality Leadership & Educational Leadership

Courses Taught:
- Group psychology of organizations
- Interview and observation in organizations
- Group relations and organizational diagnosis
- Experimental group dynamics

Supervision in organizational psychology

Prominent Theories:
- Alderfers Motivational Theory

Illustration of diverse works:
- Examination of article on Asian American and Leadership.
- Questions raised about corporate directors assessment of chief executives.
- Field experiments conducted examining race relations embedded in organizations.
- Biography of Henry(Hank) W. Riecken, a prominent applied behavioral scientist.

Maslow's Hierarchy of Needs

Maslow's hypothesis follows that every human being has a hierarchy of five needs.

1.) Physiological—associated with shelter, food, sex & other bodily needs.
2.) Safety—Protection from physical and emotional harm.
3.) Social—affection, friendships, relationships, belonging...
4.) Esteem—self respect, status, achievement and so forth.
5.) Self Actualization—drive to strive to reach ones potential. Relating to self-fulfillment. Maslow further separated these needs into lower & higher order needs. Lower order needs are those satisfied externally (physiology & safety).

Higher order needs are satisfied internally (social, esteem & self actualization).

Herzberg's Two—Factor Theory

Also referred to as the motivation—hygiene theory. Emphasizes the individuals attitude toward work as playing a critical role in determining success or failure of the task at hand.

Key question of theory:

What do people want from their jobs?

Herzberg concluded that results were significantly different when people felt good about their jobs as opposed to negative perceptions.

1.) Proposed notion of "satisfaction vs. No satisfaction".
2.) pointed out importance of conditions surrounding the job, e.g. work relations, job security, compensation etc. Herzberg called these factors Hygiene Factors.

McGregor's Theory X and Theory Y

Presents two distinct views of human beings.

Theory X (Negative)—implies managers hold four assumptions

1.) Employees inherently dislike work, will avoid work whenever possible.
2.) Following assumption 1, employees must therefore be forced , threatened in order to achieve goals.
3.) Employees will avoid responsibilities and seek formal direction.
4.) Employees place security over factors associated with work. (show little ambition.)

Theory Y (Positive)

1.) Work viewed as natural as rest or play
2.) Self—direction and control utilized by employees when committed to objective.

3.) Average person capable of learning and seeking/accepting responsibility.

4.) Decision making widespread within population, not just function of managers.

Vroom's Expectancy Theory

States that "the strength of a tendency to act in a certain way depends on the strength of an expectation that the act will be followed by a given outcome and on the attractiveness of that outcome to the individual".

Employee standpoint: He or She will be motivated to give their best effort toward a specific task when they believe their efforts will be rewarded with the greatest recognition whether through a bonus or other recognition by the organization.

Three main areas of focus:

1. Effort-performance relationship which deals with individual perception.

2. Performance-reward relationship relates to the extent of individuals belief that they will be rewarded.

3. Rewards-personal goals relationship pertains to the attractiveness of rewards to individuals.

Paul Hersey and Ken Blanchard's Situational Theory (SLT)

Description: A contingency theory that focuses on the followers readiness.

Main Points:

1. Successful leadership is achieved by selecting the right leadership style.

2. Theorists argue that this successful leadership is contingent on the level of the followers readiness.

Why focus on the *followers*?

Emphasis on the followers in leadership effectiveness reflects reality in that it is the followers who accept or reject the leader. Regardless of what the leader does, the end result depends on the actions of his or her followers.

Readiness defined: Extent to which people have ability and willingness to accomplish a specific task.

Leader—Follower relationship: SLT views this relationship similar to a parent/child relationship. As the child becomes more mature and responsible, the parent needs to relinquish control of the child to a degree.

Four key behaviors of SLT:

1.) Followers Unable and Unwilling : Leader needs to give clear and specific directions.

2.) Unable and Willing: Leader displays high task orientation to compensate for followers lack of ability, also has to get followers to buy into his/her desires.

3.) Able and Unwilling: Leader employs supportive and participative style.

4.) Able and Willing: Leader does not do much.

Concluding Remarks:

- Theory has wide appeal with management specialists, used at over 400 of the Fortune 500 companies.

- Builds on logic that leaders can compensate for ability and motivation limitations in their followers.

- Research efforts to test and support theory generally disappointing, some argue due to scientific inconsistencies in methodologies.

- Even though theory is widely popular, complete endorsement of this theory is cautioned against.

Ohio State Studies

Most comprehensive of behavioral theories from Ohio State University research that began in the late 1940s. Study identified two categories:

1.) Initiating Structure: extent to which a leader is likely to define and structure his or her role and those of subordinates in the search for goal attainment. It points to behavior such as assigning group members to particular tasks, expectations of workers to abide outlined standards and the critical role of deadlines.

2.) Consideration: Leader exhibits job relationships by showing concern for followers comfort, well being, status and satisfaction. Such a leader helps employees with personal issues, is friendly, personable, and approachable and treats employees equally.

Research Findings:

- Leaders high on initiating structure and consideration tend to achieve high employee performance and satisfaction.

- Leaders behavior focusing on initiating structure led to greater grievances, absenteeism, etc.

- High consideration negatively related to performance ratings of leader by his/her superiors.

University of Michigan Studies

Leadership studies conducted by U. of Michigan survey research center.

Objective: Locate behavioral characteristics of leaders that appeared to be related to measures of performance effectiveness.

Two main dimensions of leadership behavior:

1.) Employee Oriented Leader—emphasizes on interpersonal relationships.

2.) Production Oriented Leader—emphasizes on technical or task aspects of the job. Main concern is accomplishing group tasks.

Conclusion: Employee-oriented leaders associated with higher group productivity and higher job satisfaction.

Edwin Locke's Goal Setting Theory

1.) Emphasizes the importance of outlining specific goals to shoot for vs. generalized notions such as "do your best". Clear goals in turn will yield better results and performance.

2.) Intentions to work toward a goal are a major source of work motivation.

3.) Difficult goals if accepted result in higher performance than easier goals. (ability & acceptance being held constant). Acceptance of a difficult goal means an employee will do their best until the goal is achieved, lowered or abandoned.

4.) Feedback leads to higher performance than non—feedback. People will do better when they get feedback on how well they are performing. Feedback also helps point out what needs to be worked on.

5.) The more specific a goal, the more it triggers the internal mechanism.

Other factors influencing the goal setting theory:

A). Goal commitment—level of individuals commitment toward goal.

B). Adequate self-efficacy—individuals belief that he/she is capable of performing task. Individuals with high self-efficacy will try harder in difficult situations than those with low self-efficacy. Similarly, individuals with high self-efficacy will respond better to negative feedback.

C). Task characteristics—goals more attainable when simple rather than complicated.

D). National culture—better suited cultures than others.

Remarks:

Intentions through hard and specific goals are a great motivating force that could lead to higher performance under ideal conditions, however, no evidence exists associating this notion with higher job satisfaction. Issues pertaining to participatory set goals have mixed results.

Non-charismatic Theories

Theory has three main components:

1.) Stresses symbolic and emotionally appealing leader behaviors.

2.) Explains how certain leaders are able to achieve exceptional levels of followers commitment.

3.) De-emphasizes theoretical complexities and looks at leadership from the "average person" point of view.

Description: states that followers make attributions of heroic or extraordinary leadership abilities when observing certain behaviors. This is primary in distinguishing charismatic vs. un-charismatic leaders.

Related Studies: identifies five main characteristics of such leadership.

A.) Vision

B.) Willingness to undertake risks.

C.) Sensitivity to environmental constraints

D.) Sensitivity to follower needs

E.) Show behaviors that are out of ordinary

How do charismatic leaders influence followers?

Leaders articulates appealing vision, this vision then provides a sense of community for the followers by empowering them with better expectations with the organization. Leader follows up by communicating high performance expectations and reinforces confidence that followers can achieve these goals, which in turn builds follower self-confidence & esteem. Finally, the charismatic leader undertakes self sacrifices and engages in unconventional behavior.

Research Opinions:

Shows impressive correlation between charismatic leadership and performance levels. Most experts also contend that charismatic leadership can be a learned trait through training. Experts also conclude that charismatic leadership is not a pre-requisite in achieving high performance levels.

Organizational Behavior Concepts:

7.4 Self-managed vs. cross-functional teams

Self-managed teams typically consist of 10-15 members who perform interdependent jobs/tasks. Such teams also assume the responsibility of their former supervisors such as planning, scheduling, operating decisions, and so forth. Self-managed teams also select their own members and evaluate each others performance, therefore reducing or eliminating the role supervisory positions. Some of the drawbacks to such teams include negative results associated with the independent nature, high levels of turn over and high absenteeism levels.

Cross-functional teams on the other hand are made up of employees drawn from similar hierarchal levels but from different work groups, departments, zones, etc. Task force groups and committees are some examples of cross-functional teams. Drawbacks of such teams include, the difficulty to manage, the length of time it takes to build trust and how time consuming they can be due to the diversity of group members.

7.5 "Ineffective communication is the fault of the sender." Do you agree or disagree?

I disagree with the statement because ineffective communication can be a function of both the sender or the recipient depending on the situation. While the sender can cause ineffective communication in some cases, the recipient may be at fault as well in some cases, for instance receivers may engage in selective perception where they choose to hear or see what they want hear/see based upon their needs, motivations, self-interests, background, and so forth therefore resulting in ineffective communication. Different interpretations of language on the part of both the sender or recipient can result in ineffective communication as well. A recipient overwhelmed with information overload may also cause ineffective communication by ignoring or overlooking certain information. Defensiveness on both the sender or receivers part can also result in ineffective communication. Finally, the sender can cause ineffective communication by filtering information to make it more favorable to their motives or goals. So essentially, ineffective communication can be the fault of the sender or the receiver depending on the situation.

7.6 How can an outsider assess an organization's culture?

- Extensive homework and research on organization by talking with former employees, friends, and other associates.
- Consulting with professional groups is also critical as is obtaining as much information about the organization through article and media.
- Researching articles about organization in publications and online sources
- Physical surroundings offers significant clues of overall organization.
- Observing and paying attention to dress codes, office furnishings, personal behaviors, is also helpful. etc.
- Observing general outlook of employees, i.e. casual, serious, sad, and so forth
- Observing and asking what formal rules are in place within the organization.
- Not to be overlooked is the importance asking a variety of questions such as the organizational background, job descriptions, etc.

Four cultural types and the characteristics of employees who fit best with each

a). Networked culture:

In this type of organization, members are viewed as family and friends. Strong bonds exist, people know each other well and like each other as well. There is greater willingness to help those in need and communication of information is very open. A major drawback with this type of culture lies in the fact that the focus on friendships can lead to poor performance and creation of cliques. Employees better suited to this culture tend to be very sociable and have low solidarity qualities.

b). Mercenary culture:

Such organizations are extremely goal oriented/focused. People within the organization are very intense and determined to meet goals. Getting things done quickly is a top priority, people also have strong sense of purpose. Winning is critical even if it takes destroying those deemed as enemies. Little socialization occurs within such organizations and tolerance for low performers is very thin. This type of organization is better suited for individuals who are low on sociability and high on solidarity

c). Fragmented culture:

This is an organization comprised of individualists. Commitment to the individual and his/her job tasks is the first priority. Little or no identification with the organization exists. Employees are judged purely on their individual productivity and quality. A drawback with such a culture is the level of excessive critiquing of other members and the absence of camaraderie. This organization is better suited for individuals low on sociability and low on solidarity.

d). Communal culture:

This type of culture has a high regard for friendship and performance. A high sense of belonging and togetherness exists, however, there is also intense focus on goal achievement. The leadership of such groups typically is inspirational and charismatic while maintaining a clear vision of the organizational direction and future. This culture has a tendency of following a cult like structure as the followers take on the role of disciples to the leader. This culture is ideal for those high on sociability and high on solidarity.

7.7 Dr. Edward W. Deming(1900-1993): Icon of Management Thought.

In today's global economy, survival of business entities is contingent upon maintaining a competitive edge , constantly reconfiguring the organizational structure, goals, positioning , strategy, and philosophy. Non-so evident is the rise of the Asian markets as a force to be reckoned with in global economics. Prior to the 1950's, the aforementioned Asian markets were merely a laughable joke in the world of global economics. The Asian markets, in particular Japan owes its economic success to a relatively mildly known scholar by the name of Edward Deming. Prior to taking this course, one could have posed the question, who is Edward Deming?, and without doubt my mind would have drawn a blank response. Such is the tale of Dr Edward W. Deming. Obscure outside the world of management thought yet so instrumental to the field as a whole. For a vast majority, the name would be no different from just another John Doe, however reality presents a more intriguing perspective to this man so often referred to as The Man of contemporary management thought. To quote a famous phrase, there is more than meets the eye, with regard to this man and his contributions to management theory and global economics. Thus said, this review attempts to present an objective look and overview of Dr Edward W. Deming, the paper will outline his background and explore his contributions to the field of Organizational Behavior and Management. Special mention and thanks are afforded to Dr Donald A. Forrer my course instructor and academic advisor for his instrumental role in introducing me to the field of organizational behavior as relates to prominent Theorists within the field.

Historical Background

Dr Edward W. Deming was born, on October 14, 1900 in Sioux City, Iowa.(1900-1993) His early life was consumed by poverty and an underprivileged upbringing.[1] The setting of his family structure was a four-room tar paper shack where worry about their next meal was a constant part of their daily regime. Under such uncompromising confines, it was perhaps what shaped Deming to an icon he would later prove to be.[2] At the tender age of 8, Deming embarked on menial jobs out of necessity to help out the family financial woes and by age 17 having gathered up some savings, he enrolled at the University of Wyoming studying engineering, he would later progress to Yale University where he earned a Ph.D. in mathematical physics in 1927. [3] Despite being offered several offers in the private sector, Deming opted to take up a position with the Department of Agriculture in Washington D.C. where he would eventually meet his future wife. The real story of Deming however begins in the 1950s when he is introduced to Japanese officials. Prior to meeting with the Japanese, Deming had proposed his TQM theory but all his efforts were to no avail at home, his theory was widely rejected. During this period, Japan was just emerging from World War II and was in the mist of exploring all options of rebuilding, the Japanese took notice of Demings theory and the two parties met. This meeting of Deming and the Japanese would have unimaginable consequences.[4] It is important to point out that at this time, Deming was virtually an unknown.

An important factor to the success of this partnership was the Japanese willingness to listen, learn and make adjustments to their existing management styles to accommodate the teachings of Deming. As one source would put it, [5] The Union of Japanese Scientists which had sought out Deming listened as he taught them, and transformed their reputation for manufacturing from laughable to laudable. [6] For the next thirty years, Deming would devote his time working with the Japanese, it wasn't until the 1980's that the NBC network brought him to light in America through a documentary. The thirty relationship between the parties would forever transform the Japanese business sector and transform it to a premier force.

Prominent Theories & Contributions to the field.

a) Total Quality Management

Without any dispute , this is the theory that put Deming on the map of global economics. Today the theory is a buzzword and mainstay in the business circles, business curricular, and the global economy. Taken at face value, the theory seems bland and everyday commonsense, in fact some critics have gone as far as arguing that this theory has long being a part of the business world and Deming merely exported it to Japan and is unduly credited. However persuasive the arguments, what cannot be disputed is the critical role Deming played in bringing the theory to prominence and staking its place as a mainstay. The contemporary management thought defines Total Quality Management (TQM) as, [6] A philosophy of management that is driven by the constant attainment of customer satisfaction through the continuous improvement of all organizational processes. This definition is in constant conflict with the notion of re-engineering, however the two concepts have distinctive differences despite having striking similarities. The concept of Total Quality Management can be summed up in seven steps outlined below,[7]:

1. Intense focus on the customer
2. Concern for continuous improvement
3. Improvement in quality of everything the organization does
4. Accurate measurement
5. Empowerment of employees

The notion of continuous improvement is the cornerstone of the TQM theory and is synonymous with all its elements. The theory contends that, [8] good is not good enough and criticizes managers who accept levels of performance below perfection. One of the key elements of TQM as earlier stated lies in achieving continuous improvement whilst constantly seeking to reduce or eliminate variability. Through the reduction or elimination of these inconsistencies, the theory seeks to achieve higher yields and higher quality. TQM is also critical of managers setting short-term goals, instead it encourages managers to perpetually strive for non-stop improvement and avoid being satisfied with short-term achievements. Another key element to the success of the theory was the incorporation of statistical data tools to precisely measure and project the life cycle of a particular production cycle. By employing such statistical projections, Deming was able

to follow the flow of production and constantly enhance it in order to achieve the highest yields, quality and efficiency. In addition, Deming felt by using statistical data, he was able to pinpoint errors in the production cycle and promptly fine-tune such glitches, therefore allowing him to keep a competitive age .

The constant pressure of continuous improvement would shift the focus of TQM from quality to producing large volumes of quantity at rapid speeds using specialization techniques. [9] Due to this change of direction, TQM saw a rise and prominence of quality inspectors as a direct consequence of the rapid production process. The process of TQM follows guidelines[10]:

- Quality is to satisfy agreed customer requirements continuously
- Total quality is to achieve quality at a low cost
- TQM is to obtain total quality by involving everyone's daily commitment

Successful implementation of the TQM process is contingent on following these steps outlined by Deming consisting of four principles and eight concepts.[11]

Principles

1. Delight Customer
2. Management by fact
3. People based management
4. Continuous improvement

Concepts

1. Customer satisfaction
2. Internal customers are real
3. All work is a process
4. Measurement
5. Teamwork
6. People make quality
7. Preventions
8. Continuous improvement cycle

The stages implementing successful TQM are outlined in four steps below[12]

1. Identification and preparation
2. Management understanding and commitment
3. Scheme for improvement
4. New initiative, new target and critical thinking

The techniques for suggested for successful TQM achievement are as follows[13]

1. Customer perception surveys
2. Cost of quality statement
3. Steering group
4. Quality coordinator
5. Top team workshops
6. Total quality seminars
7. Departmental purpose analysis

8. Quality training

9. Communication technique

10. Improvement action team

11. Task force

13. Quality circles

14. Suggestion schemes

15. Help calls

16. Visible data

17. Process management

18. Statistical process control

19. Process capability

20. Fool proofing

21. Just in time

b) The Fourteen Points condensed [14]

1. Adopt a new philosophy

2. Stop practice of buying at lowest prices

3. Institute leadership

4. Eliminate empty slogans

5. Eliminate numerical quotas

6. Institute on the job training

7. Drive out fear

8. Eliminate barriers between departments

9. Take action to accomplish change

10. Constant improvement

11. Cease dependency on mass production

12 Create Purpose

13. Allow workmanship

14. Constant Retraining.

c). The Seven Deadly Sins [15]

1. Lack of consistency

2. Emphasis on short-term goals

3. Evaluations

4. Mobility of top mgt

5 Depending solely on numbers to run organization

6. Excessive medical costs

7. Excessive costs of warranty

Literary Contributions:[16 & 17]}

Books:

- The New Economist (his final book)
- Out of Crisis

Articles:

- Over 171 articles and papers

Books about Dr Deming:

- Various books detailing his teachings as well as biographical books, a few include,
- Deming: The way we new him
- Deming Management at work
- Demings profound changes: when will the sleeping giant awake
- The Keys to excellence: The Story of Deming

Other Contributions and Influences:

- The W, Edwards Deming Institute (WEDI)

a non-profit organization founded by Dr Edward Deming in 1993. Its main purpose was to share and teach the Deming concepts.

- The Deming Cooperative
  provides information, programs, conferences, seminars and so forth utilizing the Deming teachings.
- Hundreds of consulting groups utilizing his principles
- His concepts are widely use in everyday curriculums.

Conclusion

Edward Deming The Man as he is so widely referred to by management scholars clearly has had a huge impact on today's and future generations. Most notable is the recognition of him being the father of the Japanese economic machine, which is today envied by many nations. His TQM teachings clearly had a dramatic impact on the Japanese business structure and are very much a part of the U.S. business structure. The success of the TQM theory transforming a war torn country from ravages and as a mere laughing stoke in the business world speaks volumes for this theory. Its continued appeal and in some cases , over-commercialization just goes to illustrate the impact Dr. Deming created. However, it is important to point out that Dr Demings legacy stretches beyond the TQM theory. Prior to his passing, he was widely sought for consultations, was bestowed numerous awards, and his teachings continue to be a part of everyday business. Demings theories have virtually spurned a cottage industry based on his teachings.

It goes without saying that Demings theory has its share of negatives, The most troubling aspect I uncovered in my research was related to TQM in its quest of constantly pushing managers to the envelop and making them not satisfied, but to keep pushing the wheel constantly. A negative consequence of this behavior is, it could lead managers to be stressed out and burnt out, and it could also make managers have a sense of under appreciation for smaller daily accomplishments. I also find the theories total disregard for short-term goals misleading. The overall benefits however clearly outweigh the negatives

and Dr Demings contribution to the field can only be summed up as remarkable and his place in history is fittingly as an Icon to Management Thought.

REFERENCE NOTES

1. Dobyns, Lioyd. 1990. <u>Deming wants big changes and he wants them fast. Smithsonian</u>
2. Dobyns, Lioyd. 1990. <u>Deming wants big changes and he wants them fast. Smithsonian</u>
3. Dobyns, Lioyd. 1990. <u>Deming wants big changes and he wants them fast. Smithsonian</u>
4. Dobyns, Lioyd. 1990. <u>Deming wants big changes and he wants them fast. Smithsonian</u>
5. Dobyns, Lioyd. 1990. <u>Deming wants big changes and he wants them fast. Smithsonian</u>
6. Robbins, Stephen P. 2001. <u>Organizational Behavior</u>, 9th ed, pg 15 & 451-53
7. Robbins, Stephen P. 2001. A <u>Organizational Behavior</u>, 9th ed, pg 15 & 451-53
8. Robbins, Stephen P. 2001. A <u>Organizational Behavior</u>, 9th ed, pg 15 & 451-53
9. Kanji, Gopal K; Asher, Mike, Understanding <u>Total Quality Management</u>, Total Quality Management, 1993 Supplement Advances, Vol. 4 Issue
10. Kanji, Gopal K; Asher, Mike, Understanding <u>Total Quality Management</u>, Total Quality Management, 1993 Supplement Advances, Vol. 4 Issue
11. Kanji, Gopal K; Asher, Mike, Understanding <u>Total Quality Management</u>, Total Quality Management, 1993 Supplement Advances, Vol. 4 Issue
12. Deming, Edward, <u>Out of Crisis,</u> MIT/CAES, 1986
13. Kanji, Gopal K; Asher, Mike, <u>Understanding Total Quality Management Total Quality Management</u>, 1993 Supplement Advances, Vol. 4 Issue
14. Deming, Edward, <u>The New Economics</u> (2nd edition) MIT/CAES, 1994
15. Kanji, Gopal K; Asher, Mike, <u>Understanding Total Quality Management,</u> 1993 Supplement Advances, Vol. 4 Issue
16& 17   The Deming Institute (WEDI) MIT Deming Institute.

SUSIKU AKAPELWA

CHAPTER VII
Intercultural Communication

8.1 Overview and Objectives

This section will present the student with intercultural communication on a broader scale in context to how this plays in this new global environment. The student will be introduced to issues relating to value differences, religious beliefs, verbal and non-verbal communication, language issues, enculturation and many more concepts. The key area of intercultural communication is gaining a firm understanding how different cultures factor into the communication process while at the same time having an awareness, respect of cultures, beliefs and attitudes different from what one is accustomed to. This is a fascinating area of study and much of what a student makes of it is a learning curve, in studying intercultural communications they are no right or wrong answers but rather intellectual insights.

8.2 Importance of intercultural communication in the 21st centaury

The 21st centaury has brought us many new ideas and transformations. Indeed in some cases this centaury has exposed us to new worldviews that once were a world apart from what we were accustomed to, and as we take a closer look at these new dimensions it is clear that at times such changes can be overwhelming as much as they could be interesting as well. We find ourselves rejecting or embracing such changes or in some cases shell shocked and not knowing what to make of it all. Gone are the days where our confines were uniform and the one size fits all paradigm could be applied, indeed it is not uncommon to be immersed in cultures within cultures which as pointed out earlier sometimes leads to colliding worldviews. Avoiding the aforementioned collision of worldviews is the very core and essence of intercultural communication as we traverse this 21st centaury.

Perhaps the most intriguing and paramount of such changes

in the 21st centaury as relates to intercultural communication can be attributed to the phenomenon we have come to know as globalization. This phenomenon created in part due to technological advances and ease of mobility essentially wiped out cultural boundaries as we knew them, the world through the global interconnectedness is literally a virtual global village of commerce and trade. It is not uncommon to find one in the work place sitting side by side with co-workers from Brazil, Sweden, India in an office tower in Atlanta with its headquarters in Hong Kong. Such is our world in this era of globalization.

Given our current global condition, success as measured through being a productive and active participant of this new global era requires a keen cultural awareness and a good measure of effective intercultural communication. In our current global condition intercultural communication is a bridge to many obstacles associated with understanding different cultures and dealing with worldviews that may be different from ours. Those participants that effectively utilize the tools afforded by intercultural studies will find the transition in this era fluid and are certain to rip the rewards of globalization while maintaining their own beliefs and value systems while commanding a great understanding and respect of other worldviews. As one author put it, the manifestations of globalization are here to stay and there is no undoing them, therefore each participant needs to strive a balance in dealing with this circumstance otherwise they risk developing "unicist" belief systems and harbor feelings of discontent and anger.

The changes in the 21st centaury , globalization included are very challenging and the solution is not simplistic as they involve cross cultural conflicts, worldview conflicts, civilization conflicts and so forth, however a good grasp of intercultural communication skills only enhances one being able to overcome such obstacles. The importance of intercultural communication is further evidenced by the trend of many companies today offering intercultural awareness and intercultural communication training to their employees in order to maintain and develop a more productive and effective employee in this 21st centaury.

8.3 Intercultural Communication key in international business

Intercultural communication skills are now more than ever necessary for success in international business as trade and commerce is no longer confined within national borders. In today's world most companies operate as multinational corporations with operating units all across the globe, as such the workforce is equally mobile crossing geographic borders. Thus international transactions involve a diverse group of cultures converging and facilitating such transactions, therefore it follows that those individuals who are well vested in intercultural communication skills will make for better & more effective international business professionals. A lacking of essential intercultural communication skills is likely to increase apprehensive behaviors and foster cultural conflicts & clashes particularly in this era of globalization. A positive mindset is essential in developing effective intercultural skills, such a mindset involves keeping an open mind, having patience and most important having the willingness and commitment to obtain such skills.

8.4 Potential conflicts in cross cultural dialogue

As Americans engage in negotiations with other cultures, they will certainly have to deal with conflicting issues relating to different belief systems, values, religions, attitudes, gender roles, social concepts, time concepts and all attributes that make up a given culture overall. In some cases the American culture may possess similar belief norms, however in negotiating with different cultures, a difference in view with one of the above-mentioned traits is recipe for conflict to arise during the negotiation process. Americans may also run into ethnocentric elements with the respective culture engaged in negotiations, such ethnocentric elements may also raise problems during this process of negotiation. Similarly, varying degrees of respective worldviews may present a problem during negotiations. Use of language whether verbal or nonverbal is another source of potential conflict when dealing with a different culture, closely related to this concept are time and space concepts as well.

All the above-mentioned problems could take the form of direct confrontation or in some cases indirect confrontation through third parties. Direct confrontation may result from transactional negotiations as well as conflict/dispute resolution. Another area where problems could arise is associated with the identity of a culture. Americans may run into what is referred to as "individualism vs. collectivism", this in itself could hinder the negotiation process. Other potential sources of problems could be encountered when caught up in cultural conflict related to "egalitarianism vs. Hierarchy" and "High vs. low-context communication". As we have seen several potential red flags could present a problem when negotiating with other cultures. Many more areas for potential problems during negotiations exist, these are some of the more likely and common ones.

8.5 Are People in general prepared for the increase in intercultural contact?

Indeed it is quite true as suggested by Samovar and Porter that that the dynamic of intercultural communication is more prevalent now more than ever. As the text suggests, contributing factors toward this phenomenon are things such as globalization which by its very nature brings about mobility of workers across borders and cultures. Equally important are the technological advances that have been attained such as the world wide web, satellite TV, and a host of wireless communication. Naturally this technological leap has at the very least served as an education platform for cultures to learn about each other from a distance. Another attribute to the rise in intercultural communication are immigration trends, typically relating to groups from third world countries relocating to the more affluent developed nations as they strive to seek a better livelihood. The influx of such groups can be clearly seen in N. America particularly states such as California, Texas and Florida which boost large Latino Hispanic communities.

As pointed out, the trend is undoubtedly widespread and on the rise, however despite this trend, it is my belief that most people on the contrary are not prepared for this trend particularly here in N. America where issues relating to culture and race have a rocky history and always dealt with delicately with innuendos of political correctness. Even though most people are clearly aware of this trend, they may choose to block it off and perceive it as being out of their realm and merely an infringement on their cultural values as evidenced by the large anti-immigration sentiment and more recent Islamic Christianity scrutiny as a result of ongoing conflicts. Thus said, as this dynamic continues to ensue and expound itself, one begins to see the rise of sub-cultures within greater culture. A good example of which I have first hand experience can be observed in the Miami—Dade—West Palm Beach metropolitan area, by all accounts a diverse cultural hub. From the outside, all the various ethnicities that make up this large urban area appear as a mosaic, however upon a closer look, one finds that each ethnic group creates its own self-sustaining niche based on cultural values, religion and language. As such you have bedroom communities such as Little Cuba/Hialeah with predominentantly Cubans, Little Haiti (Haitians), Lauderdale/Lauderhill/ Broward county(Jamaicans & Islanders), West Palm Beach (Jewish) and so forth. For the most part, intercultural communication is somewhat hampered as each ethnic group holds their binding common denominator dearly and weary of letting in what may be perceived as being outside the norm, thus you have a situation where communication outside the norm is out of practicality & necessity.

8.6 Worldview formation & Cultural differences

Most author's and scholars are of the assumption that worldview is implicit, implied in non-verbal expression thus it's actual formation a matter of speculation. Thus said, the formative period of worldview goes back to early childhood, in fact as early as infancy. The infant through cognitive behaviors as well as parental assertions begins to form its notion of worldview. In addition to parenting, the child's immediate environmental confines also play a vital role in the formation of a particular worldview. The author's also point to other extenuating factors such as religion/faith, social groups/class, school influences, physical environment and so forth playing a vital role in shaping worldview. Greater emphasis is placed on religion as a driving force. The argument presented by Emerson follows the notion that since religion shapes reasoning and provides meaning, importance and properness, as such Emerson asserts that since religious beliefs vary globally, it is follows people develop different worldviews. Chamberlain and Zika(1992) counter this notion and present religion as just one of many contributing factors in the formation of a worldview.

I believe there are indeed cultural differences in the process by which worldview is formed. An example would be three distinct family units on three different continents, (assume three separate families, one in each of these countries; Zambia, Columbia & Canada), all with similar religious persuasions, class, and social status. As these families evolve, the assumption being the time period and all other factor are relatively similar, each family unit would take upon it's own worldview with cultural differences playing it's part. The wide array of cultural groups across the globe in it's self perhaps is a good indication of cultural differences engrained in the mechanisms of worldview formation.

8.7 Gender differences in decoding nonverbal messages

The greater consensus seems to support the premise that woman are overwhelmingly better at decoding nonverbal messages. Several researchers such as Judith Hall(1984) through her review of numerous studies on sex differences related to nonverbal decoding skills points to the same conclusion. Similar studies by Robert Rosenthal and the likes of Knupp/Hall also point to the female gender as being the better-equipped group to decode nonverbal messages. The only exception to this inference seems to arise from recent studies conducted by Knupp and Hall(1997) where men were found to be more equipped at decoding anger cues from other men. Another point worth noting , also from the same study found no tangible differences when it came to the ability of determining whether an individual was lying simply by means of nonverbal cues.

Several theories and notions try to offer an explanation as to why women seem to have a comparative advantage as relates to decoding nonverbal signals. Rosenthal(1997) offers the reasoning that women exhibit better decoding skills than men because they tend to gaze longer at faces of those they are interacting with therefore are more adapt at picking up on nonverbal signals. The other assumption gives credit to women's experience with children particularly in motherly caregiver roles. As such, the reasoning follows; this close contact with children who for the most part communicate with nonverbal cues enhances ones capability of reading, detecting and decoding nonverbal signals. Hall(1994) on the other hand suggests that since women typically tend to be more sensitive than men, they are more likely to seek and look for nonverbal cues as a means of maintaining the harmony. Nancy Henley(1973, 1977) presents an interesting perspective centering on the theory of "oppression" which contends that since women over periods of time have been in positions that carry less power, they invariably must learn the skills to read nonverbal messages from those with power over them . I tend to agree with all the explanations presented, however I also have a theory I thought about. I think women have perhaps developed a genetic internal signal that gives them a comparative advantage developed over millions of years of evolution. The combination of all the above factors over a period of time essentially gave the female gender an advantage.

8.8 Cultural conflict as a result of differences in high & low context cultures

Differences between High and low context cultures can contribute to intercultural conflict in a variety of ways. The first such possible source of conflict can be attributed to the communication patterns within each culture. In high context cultures, we find a culture where communication is transmitted via a spiral logical configuration & nonverbal hints as well as indirect means, which is contrary to the communication patterns in low context cultures. In such cultures, we find the communication patterns follow a more direct verbal interaction compounded with a linear logical platform. Given these contradictory approaches in communication patterns within the two cultures, it would be therefore clear to see how this dimension would be a potential source of intercultural conflict.

The second potential source of conflict within the cultures relates to the cultural make up, particularly of importance the traits indicating as to whether a culture follows an individualistic or collective approach in it's day to day interactions . On the surface this seems like a narrow dimension, however when we further examine this issue we see that central to each cultural behaviors are two very divergent behaviors. In low context culture we find that this entails an individualistic ideal, which is contrary to the collectivist approach found in high context cultures, as can be seen , such a contrary view could possibly contribute to conflict. Also a difference in conflict trigger mechanisms could be a source of conflict within the two cultures, for instance the value placed on saving face in low culture is not of paramount importance in high context cultures.

8.9 Negotiation strategy & Cultural Values

Cultural values as we know entail a variety of components which may be unique from one culture to another, in addition the norms associated with each culture will vary from culture to culture thereby allowing for each culture to have it's own distinctive characteristics and belief systems. Given such a backdrop, it clear to see how a negotiator's plan could be affected. In planning for negotiations, the planner has to compensate for potential forces that may arise due to differences between individualistic vs. collective cultures otherwise risk the plan being derailed. Since the focus in individualistic cultures tend to reward individual accomplishments and generally promote autonomy of the individual, it is important to keep this in mind when dealing with cultures outside this framework as the reward mechanisms and expectations may be very different. For instance, in collective cultures, the emphasis is placed on promotion of the individual through interdependence of individuals, the team/village concept as a result is more dominant. Therefore, a negotiation plan that lacks a clear understanding of which cultural values are being addressed could be adversely affected. Similarly other cultural value issues related to egalitarianism vs. hierarchy and notions of high context vs. low context will affect the negotiation plan , thus have to be planned for as well.

8.10 Messages of Reconciliation, Assimilation and Pluralism

Messages of reconciliation are voices that reflect the center position. Such messages emphasize moderation, tolerance, accommodation, integration and balance. As such, these messages are more inclined to support notions of diversity, multiculturalism, equal rights, and so forth. The civil rights movement under Dr King portrays a good example of how a balancing act was employed to stay in the middle with non-violent protest calls. Similarly the struggles of Nelson Mandela would seem to suggest a centrist position. Proponents of this concept argue for ideological moderation and shy away from the extremities of the "left wing" and the conservative "right wing". Some go as far as to suggest that messages of reconciliation essentially represent middle America.

Messages of reconciliation relate to messages of assimilation and messages of pluralism in the sense that the messages of reconciliation functions as a buffer between the two extreme concepts. On the one hand are your messages of assimilation closely tied to the political right and on the other hand are your messages of pluralism which are associated with the extreme left both been held in balance by messages of assimilation as a bridge.

8.11 Enhancing one's level of intercultural awareness

In this era of globalization and an ever-increasing interconnectedness, intercultural awareness is of paramount importance to intercultural communication. As companies more than ever operate as multinational global conglomerates, employers find themselves working across borders with people of cultures different from theirs. In addition, the effects of globalization have resulted in the influx of cross-migration as new immigrants seek new opportunities. Given all these manifestations of globalization and the new global economy, it is apparent to see that those individuals who possess a full grasp of cultural awareness through comprehension and understanding of other cultures will have a comparative advantage in this new global economy. Essentially, people in this group will tend to be more effective in understanding and communicating with other cultural groups therefore being better and more effective in the workplace and their respective fields. In addition people who are more culturally aware will tend to be more respectful, tolerant and understanding of worldviews different from what they are accustomed to which is a critical and invaluable trait. The importance of intercultural awareness is further substantiated by the increased number of cultural awareness seminars & training programs offered by corporations today.

8.12 Haitian Culture: case study analysis

This review is centered on the Haitian Culture as a people in reference to the partial fulfillment of the requirements to Pol6631 Intercultural Communications. The review looks at the culture as a whole by analyzing dynamics such as language, religion, gender roles and so forth. A brief narrative of the historical perspective opens up the case study pointing to the founding of the island, colonialism, post-independence to present day Haiti. As the paper manifests, we will be able to see that Haitian Culture is unlike any other in the western hemisphere, which makes it so fascinating as a Term paper case study.

One such interesting dynamic of this particular culture pertains to it's location in the western hemisphere; here we find a cultural group with African root's via the slave trade that is clearly distinct from other such groups in North America, South America & the greater Caribbean Islands. The most perplexing of such contrasts one finds lies in the linguistic traits. Most descendants of this manifestation adopted the English, Spanish or Portuguese tongue as their primary means of verbal communication, however such is not the case with Haiti where the Creole language evolved, even though bearing a resemblance to the French language, it is still clearly not mutually tied to French and holds it's own distinctive verbal and written characteristics. Another interesting perspective to this culture lies in it's religious convictions, Catholicism and a segment of Protestant beliefs plays a major role, however we find another dynamic segment known as Voodoo which plays a major role as a faith in this culture. The close ties to Witch Craft and indigenous African Native faiths presents an interesting view. These are some of the few interesting perspectives this paper will examine as earlier pointed out.

Historical Overview

The Island of Haiti was discovered by the explorer Christopher

Columbus during his voyages in the late 1400's. The Island also referred to as the Island of Hispaniola, which encompasses Haiti and Dominican Republic, both sharing the geographic landmass as neighbors. The Island was initially inhabited by the Taiw Indian's who called their homeland as Ayti or Hayti which translates to "mountains" as is characterized by the topography of the Island.[1.] The Indian native population would be virtually eliminated by the mid 1500's by virtue of disease, abuse and forced labor.

The Haitian historical time lime would follow several paths since it's discovery by Columbus. First ensued the Spanish discovery and Colonialization followed by French colonialization. The Spanish era began with about 2000 Spaniards who had about 30,000 African Slaves who were brought in to replace the decimated Indians. The French era was established in 1659 primarily playing a greater part was the French West India company. [2.] This period was driven by the sugar and coffee interests on the Island. Essentially the slave trade as a labor source to the aforementioned trade of sugar & coffee fostered this period. The inhabitation of African Slaves on the Island grew to over 500,000 by 1681[3.]

Following this period came the Haitian revolution also called the Slave rebellion in 1791 culminating in the Haitian Independence. U.S. occupation occurred between 1915—1934. The state since followed a string of military governments during the Papa Doc and Baby Doc era's. The state has struggled to have any stable governing body and has been plagued by instability, human abuses and widespread poverty. Today the Island is inhabited by about 7 million people primarily black African slave descendants with a minority population of mixed raced descendant's(5%) also known as Mulattos. The Principal city is Port au Prince with close to 800,000 people representing over 61 percent of the total urban population. [4].

Language dynamics

Two primary languages are spoken in Haiti, the main language spoken by over ninety percent of the population is Creole and a smaller segment speak French or both. This duality of languages has resulted in an interesting cultural dilemma. Typically all Haitians across the spectrum were proud to embrace Creole as the national language and the use of French was limited to the elite part of society. Thus said, even though French was designated as an official language, it is essentially limited to very few government and commerce leaders. Here we see our first level of intercultural conflict based on language, where one use of language is associated with elitism and limited to formal settings and the other language is viewed as a lower class language.

Today however, these attitudes are far less visible as Creole has gained widespread positive perception and has been embraced by all the population as the language of choice. In fact, a sense of nationalism and pride is now associated with Creole usage.[5] The origins of the Creole language is somewhat unclear, some contend it evolved as a pidgin exchange between French colonialists and African slaves, while others contend that it came to the island as a full scale language. The former would seem logical particularly as many words in the Creole language have a French origin even though the two languages are no mutually comprehensible. [6.] It is also important to point out that Creole is not a dialect of French. One text offers the following description of Haitian Creole as follows: "autonomous language based on 17th century lexical French and on syntax principles of west African languages." [7].

For a good period of time, the Creole language had no written form, the first attempts to put Creole in written form were first conceptualized and materialized in the 1940's by an Irish Methodist minister known as H. Ormond McConnell and his companion a renowned American literacy specialist known as Frank Laubach. The two developed a written version based on the international phonetic alphabet.[8]. A new dynamic is evolving in present day Haiti as a result of mass migration of Haitians to north America, particularly south Florida and New York. Many Haitians now are more inclined to learn the English language out of practicality as they hold on to dreams of making it to North America, as such the use of English is growing in Haiti.

Religion

Roman Catholicism today is the official religion of Haiti, this religion gained ground after the Haitian revolution. Prior to the revolution plantation owners did not want religious education to the slaves in fear of their control being compromised. In fact in 1764 the plantation owners expelled the Jesuits for trying to spread the gospel.[9]. Eventually the religious evangelists primarily from Europe would penetrate the island and continue to spread the gospel. This spread of Christianity also involved attempts to eliminate ritualistic practices such as the widely practiced voodoo. Today, people in Haiti devote a good portion of their life to practicing religion, indeed unlike most other groups, Haitian people seem very faithful and committed to their Christian faiths. In my interviews and testimonials with the Haitian community here in south Florida, one common denominator as I conducted interviews from one family to another was the unquestionable faith to Christ, in fact I found that most everyday life was centered on work, family and the church. A smaller segment of the Haitian people(15-25%) follow protestant, Baptist and Methodist denominations.

Perhaps the most intriguing facet of life associated with Haiti lies in the rituals of voodoo faith. A lot of misconceptions and equal fascination with voodoo has existed for a long time as seen in movie portrayals, everyday conversation and so forth. In fact, in one of my interviews and testimonial sessions with members of the Haitian community, one of the facets that was raised when I had inquired about what most people are inclined to know when the first meet someone of Haitian descent, the interviewees would give me a friendly laugh and the overwhelming consensus was people's intrigue with Haiti and voodoo, indeed I must admit, I while trying to maintain my research platform had the voodoo issue in the back of my mind. What with this voodoo question is the million-dollar question as the saying goes. Such was my quest to uncover and have a true understanding of this manifestation particularly with some of the similarities of the African cultural rituals I had witnessed as a young boy in Africa.

Voodoo has been characterized as the unofficial religion of Haiti, indeed the practice is widely engrained in the fabric of Haitian everyday society, however to garner a clear perspective of this practice, a brief look at it's origins is essential. One text describes the birth of voodoo through night ceremonies and dances by slaves . One such famous gathering occurred in the summer of 1791 led by Bois—Caymen a slave overseer and voodoo priest.[10.] Such gatherings entailed slaves from different plantations meeting at night in a secret location and proceeding in dance song and ritualistic sacrifices to the ancestors & gods, this off course unbenounced to the slave masters, anyone caught organizing or participating in such rituals was essentially risking their life. My observation of the ritualistic practices of this belief have an unparallel similarity to African rural practices with hints of witchcraft. Both ceremonies are closely tied to animal sacrificial rituals to the ancestors and spirits. The processional march to the sacrificial site filled with song and dance to fever pitch levels also draws a parallel between the two cultures. The basic assumption of this faith can be characterized as a derivative of African traditional song and dance ceremonies that placed emphasis on giving thanks to the ancestral spirits and cleansing those who were perceived to be under the spell of evil or demonic spirits. The ceremonial rituals were conducted by the "high priests" and issues pertaining to evil spirits were designated to "Witch Doctors". The central theme of this belief seems misunderstood, but at close view one can see close parallels to many religious practices just different approaches.

Gender Roles & Family Structures

The gender roles in mainstream Haiti revolve around marital relationships, typically men taking up the role of head of household and engaging in the perceived masculine chores. Women for the most part are key in domestic roles such as cooking, cleaning, etc and play a critical role in child rearing. This phenomenon is even greater in rural areas. In the urban areas men and women enter into Christian marriages with vows exchanged and so forth, however, an interesting practice occurs in rural areas where typical marital ties among the peasants follow a mutual agreement between the wife & husband to have an economic partnership, such unions are not formal recognized marriages under the Haitian law but for all practical purpose are essentially unions. Such arrangements are referred to as "Plasaj" [11]. This practice is not only isolated to rural peasants but is also practiced by the poor in urban areas who do not have the funds marriage licenses and a formal wedding ceremony . Haitian families are usually of a large size, it's not uncommon for a family unit to have five ,six, seven or more children. Aside from the mother & father roles, an integral part of the family is the extended family, it is a widespread practice for a household to have parents, children, uncles, aunts and grandparents all living under one roof. Everyone shares in the roles of raising and parental roles to the young children. Haitian life is centered on family and visiting between friends and family is a part of life and also serves as a pastime, particularly since Haiti as a third world society lacks many recreational amenities found in developed societies. It customary to offer food to guests when they come for a visit and even if one is full, it is considered rude and offensive to say no to the offer. Haitian people like many African cultures use a lot of gestures and are animated when conversing, touching, hugging & embracing are a common part of conversations, it is normal to see men talking and holding hands, laughing , embracing without any phobia.[12]. Church worship also plays a big part in Haitian life and it is customary for the whole family to attend church on Sundays. The main sport in Haiti is soccer also known as football, this by far the biggest pastime young kids engage in. Song and dance are a way of life as well, some of the Haitian rhythms closely resemble African rhythms and so does the rhythmic movements and gyrations. The education system follows a form of primary school and secondary school where students choose a concentration of subjects to focus on, students can choose science, liberal arts, mathematics etc. The staple food consists of rice usually mixed with beans, or vegetables, on weekends the rice may be eaten with chicken or beef/pork as a special treat as many cannot afford to eat as such on a regular basis. Other common foods include fish, vegetables and fruits.

Intercultural Dynamics & Interethnic Conflict

Haiti is primarily composed of three classes of people like many societies. The upper class constitutes a very small segment of about 2 percent of the total population and control's over 40 percent of the national income.[13]. This group controls most of the business sector and hold key government positions, until recently most of this segment are member's of a group referred to as Mulattos who had wealth passed from generation to generation and through marriages between elite families. The term Mulatto essentially relates to Haitian's of mixed race with a lighter skin complexion. To be part of this elite group usually entailed being able to speak French and living a lifestyle with French etiquette. Everything tied to being French epitomizes this group, from names, lifestyle, mannerisms etc.

The second group is the Middle Class, this group is slightly bigger in size compared to the upper class but still relatively small when compared to the total population. Figures from the last census data had this number at about 5 percent of total population, even though the number is a little larger today.[14]. This group is made up of a mixture of black Haitian's and Mulatto Haitian's, interestingly enough, this is where the vast majority of conflict between the blacks and Mulattos can be found as both strive to leap into the upper class. The same French aspects found with the elite upper class are also a part of the middle class. This group is made up of young professionals and government workers.

The largest segment of population falls into this final segment of lower class, over 70 percent of the total population make up this group. Rural peasants and the urban poor constitute Haiti's lower class. The rural Haitian's basically live of the land as subsistence farmers occasionally making some extra money by selling produce at the market or on roadsides. The urban poor usually do the menial work, typically involving hard labor, also in this group are beggars, vagrants and so forth.

Power Distance, Worldview & Politics

As one would expect, the Power Distance Index (PDI) in Haiti is very high as most of the power, prestige and wealth lies in very few elite hands. Haitian Culture seems to follow a religious worldview, as pointed out earlier in the paper Haitian society is closely tied to Catholicism and Voodoo beliefs. The Haitian Culture also seems to be aligned as a "Being Culture", where the pace of life is slower without a rush, the concept of time follows a polychronic (P-time) dimension with less emphasis on stringent deadlines and schedules. There is also a great respect for the elderly as they are viewed as wise and a fabric to society which can be also seen in the way grandparents live with their families rather than being placed in nursing homes. Enculturation process in Haitian culture follows typical human interactions & observations. We also find widespread use of Kinesis particularly with the tendency for Haitians to use gestures and animated facial expressions in conversations. Cultural distance is virtually non-existence as everyone practically employees Creole as the language of choice. Politics are at the center of Haitian life, from colonial periods to post independence the politics of Haiti have been complicated. Post independence saw a succession of military governments with brutal dictators that ruled by fear and brutality. Attempts for traditional democratic governments all but failed resulting in military coups, rigged elections, corruption etc. In fact today is under political turmoil with demonstrations to out the current leadership. One could argue that a great deal of poverty and mismanagement in Haiti today is a consequence of bad incompetent governments.

Conclusion & Recommendations

As we draw to the close of this review, the Haitian Culture continues to fascinate and intrigue my curiosity. I must admit this research and my numerous dialogues and interactions with Haitian people has made me more educated and left me with a greater understanding of this often misunderstood culture. Haitian people are very warm and welcoming people. What I found most intriguing during the course of my research was how this culture is so similar to my own African culture. Take away the language aspect, the two cultures virtually mirror each other. The strong Christian beliefs, Voodoo (which in my culture is essentially witchcraft & traditional healers), high ethics and morality, extended family etc are facets that also play an integral part in African culture.

The research also help dispel some misconceptions I might have had of Haitian Culture. For someone contemplating a visit to Haiti from the western world, a few adjustments may be necessary but nothing extra-ordinary. Simple adjustments such as being prepared for the widespread poverty and dilapidated state of affairs, personal caution would be recommended, avoiding traveling at night as pick pockets take such opportunities to do their deeds. Also when visiting a Haitian family and you are offered food, agree to at least try even if full as this is expected in this culture. Space use in Haitian culture is also different than in western cultures, so one should expect a lot close proximity and a good amount of hugging, shaking hands during conversations. Other than that, the Haitian culture is very open and pleasant and will always treat a guest with utmost respect.

REFERENCE NOTES

1.) Haggerty, Richard A. (1989). <u>Dominican Republic and Haiti, country studies</u>. Pg 203

2.) Wilentz, Amy.(1989) <u>The RAINY SEASON, Haiti Since Duvalier</u>. Pg 74

3.) Wilentz, Amy.(1989) <u>The RAINY SEASON, Haiti Since Duvalier</u>. Pg 74

4.) United States Department of State Country Profile(2003). Retrieved from group data base
<u>www.governermentguide.com</u>
<u><http://www.governermentguide.com/></u>

5.) Haggerty, Richard A. (1989). <u>Dominican Republic and Haiti, country studies</u> pg 258

6.) Haggerty, Richard A. (1989). <u>Dominican Republic and Haiti, country studies</u>. Pg 258

7.) Savain, Roger E. (1993) <u>Haitian-Kreol in Ten Steps</u>. Pg 11

8). Savain, Roger E. (1993) <u>Haitian-Kreol in Ten Steps</u>. Pg 3

9.) Haggerty, Richard A. (1989). <u>Dominican Republic and Haiti, country studies</u>. Pg 267

10.) Haggerty, Richard A. (1989). <u>Dominican Republic and Haiti, country studies</u>. Pg 268

11.) United States Department of State Country Profile(2003). Retrieved from group data base
<u>www.governermentguide.com</u>
<u><http://www.governermentguide.com/></u>

12.) Testimonial Interview: Sam Joseph, Haitian Immigrant.

13.) United States Department of State Country Profile(2003). Retrieved from group data base
<u>www.governermentguide.com</u>
<u><http://www.governermentguide.com/></u>

14.) United States Department of State Country Profile(2003).

Annotated Bibliography: Haitian Culture

1. Wilentz, Amy.(1989) The RAINY SEASON, Haiti Since Duvalier.

The author provides an account of modern Haiti based on her experience there beginning in 1986. The author offers the day-to-day existence of Haitian people on the streets as she visits with local people in the streets of Port—au-Prince and other countryside towns. The author also gives an insight into Voodoo practices, drawing attention to the rituals and dances associated with this practice. The text also points to the role of religion in Haiti, Catholic influences and also touches on black magic practices. The author also addresses issues of ethnology, relating to the black Haitians and Mulatto Haitians. The text also discusses the peasant movement of Papaye (MPP), looks at the plight of peasants and also touches on the widespread poverty among Haitian people. The book also gives an account of historical and political background of Haiti. This text is particularly interesting and informative as it provides somewhat of a testimonial account in great detail on a variety of subjects.

2. Lawless, Robert.(1992) Haiti's Bad Press.

The stem of this book narrates the long history of bias against Haiti and Haitians by the outside world. It points to more recent stigmas relating to The Boat People, AIDS and so forth. The author offers an account to the nature of the and origins of the bias. The text presents a detailed account of the connection between France and Haiti, centering on the ethnocentrism of this relationship as well as its implications such as the linguistic class barriers between Haitians that speak French and those who only speak Creole. The book also looks at the conflict with French designated as the official language but the overwhelming population can only speak Creole. The text also deals with the curious relationship with Roman Catholicism and the Haitian masses. Voodoo is also discussed in the text.

3. Foster, Charles R; Valdman, Albert. (1984). Haiti—Today And Tomorrow.

The contributing authors begin with a look at cultural perspectives in Haiti paying attention to Labor and Sexuality in Haiti. The Social character of religion in Haiti is also examined. The book also draws on the linguistic parallels in Haiti as well as drawing attention to the Francophilia and cultural nationalism in Haiti. The family aspect of Haitian society is looked at also. Haiti's African roots and unique cultural identity and the European-oriented mulatto elite are discussed as well. The author's also look at the political issues in Haiti which are ingrained within Haitian culture, dating back to the Haitian struggle for independence from 1791—1804. The authors also address the politics of voodoo as a religion of the poor. The book also discusses the populist ideology which is at the core of the strong sentiments of cultural nationalism within Haiti. The authors also discuss Rural social structures and Creole Literacy.

4. Haggerty, Richard A. (1989). <u>Dominican Republic and Haiti, country studies</u>.

This is a volume of books prepared by the Federal Research Division of the Library of Congress under Country Studies. The manual gives an overview somewhat a country profile of Haiti from a collection of authors thus giving one a broad overview and perspective of the country and its peoples, customs, culture, economic outlook, dominant beliefs, origins, common interests, political, economic, social institutions and so forth. The book opens with the Spanish discovery and colonialization of the island of Hispaniola today occupied by Haiti and the Dominican Republic. This is followed by a look at the period of French Colonialism, followed by the Haitian Revolution, leading to Haitian independence on January 1, 1804. The United States Occupation, 1915-34 is also examined. The Society and it's environment is then examined., discussing gender roles and family, urban lower class, the language question (French and Creole). The text further examines other issues such as religion, Voodoo, etc.

5. McDannell, Colleen (2001) <u>Religions of the United States in practice</u>, vol 2

This is a 2 part volume comprised of a collection of essays that seek to examine various religious behaviors within the United States. The subject matter of interest to my research subject matter is located in the 2nd volume (chapter 29) and is narrated by

Elizabeth McAlister. The title of her segment is: "The Rite of Baptism in Haitian Voodoo", in her analysis, she basically offers a journey into the reality and rituals of the practice of voodoo. The author follows the prayer sessions through the eyes of Haitian immigrants in American communities as they go through rituals.

6. Rodman, Selden. <u>The Miracle of Haitian Art</u>.

This book is essentially dedicated to exploring the great works of Haitian artists, sculptors, etc. the text offers both a narrative as well as a pictorial display of some of the works.

<u>Other Auxiliary Resources</u>:

7. United States Department of State Country Profile(2003). Retrieved from group data base

www.governermentguide.com

8. University of Texas, Lanic site (2003) Retrieved from group data base

http://lanic.utexas.edu/lalcb/other/

9. Global Warrior site

10. Ferguson, James (1987) <u>Papa Doc, Baby Doc, Haiti and the Duvaliers</u>.

11. Trouillot, Michel-Rolph (1990) <u>Haiti State Against Nation</u>.

12. Leyburn, James G. (1980) <u>The Haitian People</u>.

13. Savain, Roger E. (1993) <u>Haitian-Kreol in Ten Steps.</u>

14. Ridgeway, James, (1994) <u>The Haiti Files, Decoding the Crisis</u>.

15. Testimonial interviews from Haitians in Miami—Dade-Broward metro area.

16. <u><http://www.haiti.org/></u>

17. <u>www.cia.gov/</u> http://www.cia.gov/

INDEX

www.ingramcontent.com/pod-product-compliance
Lightning Source LLC
Chambersburg PA
CBHW051520170526
45165CB00002B/549